MIND POWER

John Kehoe

MIND POWER

Zoetic Inc.
Training · Growing · Succeeding

Published by
Zoetic Inc.
6370 Chatham Street
West Vancouver
British Columbia
V7W 2E2
Canada

Distributed in South Africa by
Media House Publications
Box 782395, Sandton 2146
(011) 882-6237

ISBN: 0-9694059-0-1

Printed by Australian Print Group

John Kehoe

For over a decade, John Kehoe has been recognized world wide for his pioneering work in the field of mind power. In 1975 he withdrew to the wooded seclusion of the British Columbia wilderness to spend three years in intensive study and contemplation of the inner workings of the human mind. By borrowing freely from a wide variety of sources ranging from modern psychology, physics and medicine to traditional religious and spiritual teachings and applying his own shrewd observations and insights to his findings, Kehoe was able to forge the first straightforward and successful program for developing mind power. Crowds flocked to his lectures and he was soon teaching and addressing overflow audiences throughout Canada, the U.S.A., Australia, southeast Asia, and the Orient. He has been a consultant to such corporate giants as PennAir, Mobil and Dominion Life and has been the subject of numerous newspaper, radio and television interviews. John Kehoe is a dynamic speaker, and an open and easy going philanthropist respected by all those who have been exposed to his teachings.

Acknowledgements

To Joyce Hamilton, my editor and confidante, whose coaching and polishing have made this book come alive, to Jean Kotwell and Bill McIntyre who laboured over typewriter and computer long into the night, to Maarten Heilbron and Ken Slater who laid out the pages, to Dean Owen and John Larsen for their art direction and finally, to Soraya Othman my business partner and friend whose management of day to day affairs allowed me the freedom to write this book and whose insistence that "the book get done!" propelled me into action. Thank you.

John Kehoe

Table of contents

Foreword

My goal in this book is to share with you a number of important techniques I have found useful in creating new realities. I will share with you stories of how people are successfully using these techniques and show you why they work so well.

Harnessing the forces of the universe and actively participating in the creative process of making your goals happen is an exhilarating experience. This book provides you with all the tools necessary to do that; all that remains is for you to apply them.

I am excited and thrilled to introduce you to these techniques which have made such a profound impact on my life and the lives of thousands of others whom I've had the opportunity of personally instructing. Life is indeed a wonderful adventure.

John Kehoe

Part One

1. Another View of Reality

There are more things in heaven and earth than are dreamed of by mere mortal men.
Shakespeare

TO work with mind power you do not have to understand the laws of physics or how reality manifests itself, just as you don't have to understand how a carburetor works or how a spark plug fires in order to drive a car. Few of us understand automotive mechanics but that doesn't stop us from driving. Likewise, in the science of mind power, anyone can quickly and successfully master the basics and effectively put them to work in his or her life.

We begin by examining the nature of reality, especially the startling new discoveries in science over the last ten years which have helped us to understand more clearly how the mind creates its own reality. These discoveries explain why creating visualizations in our mind is not just idle day dreaming, but is a creative process which helps us direct the same energies that hold matter together, change water into steam, or cause a seed to sprout and grow.

Understanding the nature of these energies assists us in understanding the mind and shows us why inspiration, prayer, and intuition are not supernatural phenomenon at all, but follow patterns and laws which we can discover and use at our will. Like everything else in the known universe, they are governed by laws which, robbed of their scientific jargon and broken down, can be easily understood by anyone.

Let me take you on a short adventure into these new discoveries . . .

Modern physics sees the universe as a vast, inseparable web of dynamic activity. Not only is the universe alive and constantly changing, but everything in the universe affects everything else. At its most primary level, the universe seems to be whole and undifferentiated, a fathomless sea of energy that permeates every object and every act. It is all one. In short, scientists are now confirming what mystics, seers, and occultists have been telling us for thousands of years we are not separate, but part of one giant whole.

"In him we live and move and have our being."
Acts 17:28

"When a blade of grass is cut, the whole universe quivers." *ancient Upanishad saying*

Modern physics has changed our concept of the material world. Particles are no longer seen as consisting of any basic "stuff," but as bundles of energy. They may make sudden transitions "quantum leaps" behaving at times like units, yet being wavelike on other occasions. Reality is fluid. Nothing is fixed. All are patterns in constant motion; even a rock is a dance of energy. The universe is dynamic and alive and we are in it and of it, dynamic and alive ourselves.

The universe is a giant hologram

It was the invention of the enigmatic hologram that won Denis Gabor the 1947 Nobel Prize. Let's look at what a hologram is. A hologram is a process in which "the whole" is contained in each and every one of its parts. For example, a starfish is a biological hologram. If you cut the point from a starfish it will grow a new point. Not only that the point will grow a whole new starfish because the genetic imprint of the whole starfish is contained in each and every one of its parts.

I was at a holographic exhibition in Sydney, Australia several years ago in which I saw an exhibit of photographs done with holography. In one of the pictures was an image of a woman standing straight up. If you moved to the right of the picture the woman changed suddenly and was now smoking a cigarette; if you moved to the left of the picture it changed again and she had her hip thrown out in a suggestive pose. If one were to drop this holographic plate onto the floor and it shattered into pieces, each piece would reveal, not what you would expect to see - a piece of her shoe or dress or maybe her eye - but the image of the whole woman. And if you moved any one of the little pieces from side to side, you would still see her smoke that cigarette and throw out her hip. Every single one of the small pieces would have the whole picture in it.

It now appears that the nature of reality itself is holographic and that the brain operates holographically, as well. Our thinking processes seem to be identical to the primary state of the universe, and made up of all the same "stuff". The brain is a hologram interpreting the holographic universe.

How consciousness and the physical world interact is now less of a mystery: consciousness is but energy in its finest and most dynamic form. This helps explain why events are affected by what we imagine, visualize, desire, want, or fear, and why and how an image held in the mind can be made real.

These discoveries about the nature of reality can be a major force for our continued change and growth. If we know and understand that we are a part of an open and dynamic universe and that our minds play a part in constructing reality, then we can choose to live more creatively and powerfully. We can no longer stand on the sidelines watching things happen to us, for with our new understanding, we now realize that there are no sidelines to stand on, nor were there ever. Everything is affecting everything. Even our thoughts are creating our reality.

"Discovering a new theory," Einstein once said, "is like climbing a mountain, gaining new and wider views." This is what you are doing by reading this book, and soon your mental climb will be rewarded by an open and exhilarating view of your true potential.

2.

Consciousness

So think as if your every thought were to be etched in fire upon the sky for all and everything to see, for so, in truth, it is.

Book of Mirdad

I F you think of your thoughts as a reality existing side by side with what we call "the physical reality," you will be closer to understanding the unique relationship between the two.

You are living simultaneously in two worlds, two realities: the inner reality of your thoughts, emotions, and attitudes and the outer reality of people, places, things and events. Because we fail to separate these Inner and Outer worlds, we allow ourselves to become dominated by the Outer world of appearances and use the Inner world solely as a "mirror" for whatever happens to us. Our Inner world reacts constantly and because we spend all our time reacting, we never experience our power. Ironically, you begin creating your reality the day, the hour, the minute you cease ***constantly*** reacting to it.

Your inner consciousness is a powerful force whose influence is felt in every aspect of your life. It is, in fact, the major and most important part of who you are and it is the main cause of your success or failure.

Everything at its purest and deepest essence, is energy and whenever you think you are working with an immense amount of this energy in the quick, light, mobile form of thought.

Thought is forever attempting to find form, is always looking for an outlet, is always trying to manifest itself. It is the nature of thought to try and materialize into its physical equivalent. Our normal thoughts can be compared to sparks from a fire. Though they contain the essence and potential power of the flame, they normally dissipate quickly. They last only a few seconds, fly into the air, and quickly burn out.

Although a single unaided thought hasn't much power, just repeat this particular thought over and over again. Through repetition, the thought becomes concentrated and directed and its force is magnified many times. The more it is repeated the more energy and power it generates and the more readily it is able to manifest.

**Weak and scattered thoughts are
weak and scattered forces.**

**Strong and concentrated thoughts
are strong and concentrated forces.**

To illustrate this, picture a magnifying glass through which pass the sun's rays. If the magnifying glass is moved about from spot to spot the power of the sun's rays is diffused and not apparent. If, however, the magnifying glass is held still and focused correctly at the proper height, those same rays become concentrated and that diffused light suddenly becomes powerful enough to ignite a fire.

So it is with our thoughts. As you progress in your study of mind power you will learn how to develop and concentrate your thoughts so that they become much more powerful. At this point, just realize that thoughts have power in themselves. Your deeply held beliefs, your fears, your hopes, your worries, your attitudes, your desires, and each and every thought you think, all have an effect on you and others.

Most of us go through our waking hours taking little notice of our thought processes: how the mind moves, what it fears, what it heeds, what it says to itself, what it brushes aside. For the most part, we eat, work, converse, worry, hope, plan, make love, shop, play - all with minimal thought about **how** we think.

We might be far more willing to learn how to use our mental mechanisms if we imagined for a moment that for every thought we either gained a dollar or lost a dollar depending on the type of thought. Considering we think thousands of thoughts every day, this is quite a proposition. Imagine an accounting system recording our every thought and recording which type of thoughts gained us money and which ones lost us money. How diligent we would be in controlling and directing our thoughts! How enthusiastically we would create those thoughts which made us money, and avoid those which cost us money.

This is more or less what is already happening inside you, though with energy, not dollars. There **is** a big accounting system going on: it's called the universe, and no thought produced there is without its effect.

This world of ours is no dead pile of brick and stone. It is a living, dynamic system of energy. Every thought you think impresses itself upon this system and its effect is felt. You are forever creating your reality through what you are thinking.

The beginning step to a new and more successful life is absurdly easy. You have only to pay attention to the flow of thoughts going on inside yourself and direct it accordingly. Your life can be entirely of our own making, yet look at the way you are living. You claim you want financial abundance, yet you are constantly bemoaning your lack of money and how expensive things are. You dwell on what you don't have and the bills coming in. You worry and wonder how you will get along. You may want financial abundance, but because your consciousness is of lack and worry, you will never experience that abundance.

Or maybe you wish you could find a new job, something interesting and challenging, that would use your creativity and pay you well. If you constantly tell yourself these jobs are impossible to find, it will never happen, it is very unlikely it ever **will** happen.

Perhaps you wish you could be a more outgoing individual, bold and spontaneous, full of assurance and confidence, yet you constantly focus on your inferiorities and inadequacies and put yourself down, reminding yourself again and again of your problems. You may **want** strength, but if your consciousness is of weakness, you are fooling yourself to think you will ever possess that strength.

In short, **wanting something badly will not make it happen.** Hoping for something different will have no effect. Working hard 12 to 15 hours a day is wasting your time. You will always remain where you are unless - and it's a big "unless" - **you change your thinking.**

> "To them that hath . . . more shall be given. To them that hath not, even what little they have will be taken away." *Luke 19:26*

When I first read this quote from Scripture, I didn't think it was fair. It didn't seem fair that "them that had" would get more and "them that had not" would lose what little they had. It just didn't seem right. I thought it would be more just if "them that had not" were given more, but that is not what the Scripture says. That is not the law, nor is it the way the universe works. Upon reflection I realized that what could be more fair than every person's freedom to choose for himself or herself thoughts which will, in turn, create their reality?

Want to change your circumstances? Develop the necessary consciousness. A successful person has a success consciousness. A wealthy person has developed a prosperity consciousness and his thoughts are on abundance, success, and prosperity. This is how **he** thinks.

"Easy for him," you say. "When you're successful it's easy to think success and when you're wealthy it's easy to think prosperity, but my situation is totally different. I'm not successful; I'm not wealthy. The situations and circumstances of my life keep me down."

WRONG! Dead wrong! Your circumstances and situations never keep you down. The only things that keep you down and keep you stuck are your thoughts. With work and practice you can learn to direct your thoughts and create any consciousness you choose. Your reality will change only **after** you've developed your new consciousness, not before. **The new consciousness must come first.**

What is it that you want in your life? Do you know? More health? Then get health consciousness. More power? Then get power consciousness. More prosperity? Get prosperity consciousness. More happiness? Get happiness consciousness. More spirituality? Get spiritual consciousness. Everything exists as a possibility. All that's required is for you to feed in the necessary energy until it becomes yours.

How reassuring to think that no matter what a person's past or present situation, or how many times they've previously failed, if they would but regularly feed their consciousness their situation would change! This remarkable ability has been given to each and every one of us to use or to ignore. It costs no money. It takes no special talent. It takes only the decision on your part to take the time and put forth the necessary effort to develop the appropriate consciousness. That's all! Everything else will automatically fall into place.

Your mind is like a garden which can be cultivated or neglected and you are its master gardener. You can cultivate this mind, or you can ignore it and let it develop whatever way it will. But make no mistake: you will reap the harvest of your work or your neglect!

Your mind creates your reality. You can choose to accept this or not. You can be conscious of it, and get your mind working for you, or you can ignore it, and allow it to work in ways that will hinder and hold you back. But your mind will always, and forever be creating your reality.

3.

Visualization

There is no thought in my mind but it quickly tends to convert itself into a power and organizes a huge instrumentality of means.

Emerson

WHAT is it that makes a person a winner? What distinguishes those who succeed from those who fail?

"It's all in the mind," says movie star and body builder Arnold Schwarzenegger. A multi-millionaire, successful real estate tycoon, movie star, body builder, five time winner of Mr. Universe, Arnold has it made. But it wasn't always so. Arnold can remember back when he had nothing except a belief that his mind was the key to getting where he wanted to go.

"When I was very young, I visualized myself being and having what it was I wanted. Mentally I never had any doubts about it. The mind is really so incredible. Before I won my first Mr. Universe, I walked around the tournament like I owned it. The title was already mine. I had won it so many times in my mind that there was no doubt I would win it. Then when I moved on to the movies, the same thing. I visualized myself being a successful actor and earning big money. I could feel and taste the success. I just knew it would all happen."

Chris Poellein was a member of the world renowned West German freestyle ski team which won the European Cup six times between 1976 and 1982.

"Part of our training program involved working with a psychologist to increase the power of our minds. After training on the slopes we were placed in a state of meditation and encouraged to totally repeat the slope runs in our minds, visualizing each bump and movement of the routine. We worked as hard training mentally as we did physically. Excellence in athletics - or indeed any endeavor - depends primarily on having a clear mental picture of that activity."

Chris should know, she not only has her six medals, but she now has her own successful consulting firm teaching business and sports groups how they, too, can benefit from the same techniques.

Bryan Edwards, one of Australia's top life insurance salesmen, a man of infectious good humour and spirits, spends 10 minutes every evening before he goes to bed running over in his mind his next day's calls. He pictures himself making his presentation to each client. He sees them being receptive and gladly taking out a policy with him. He imagines a very productive day with lots of sales. He does this for 10 minutes before he goes to bed and 10 minutes upon rising in the morning - a total of 20 minutes each day. Bryan Edwards sells more insurance in one week than most people do in six months.

Three totally different people with totally different goals and objectives in life, yet all are using the same technique to create and influence their reality - the technique of visualization.

Visualization is using your imagination to see yourself in a situation that hasn't yet happened, picturing yourself having or doing the thing you want, and successfully achieving the results you desire.

For example, let us say you want to be more confident. Using visualization you picture yourself as confident. You see yourself doing things, talking to people, all with confidence. You picture yourself in situations that normally give you difficulty and you see yourself in these situations at ease, confident, and performing well. You might picture your friends and associates complimenting you, congratulating you on your new-found confidence. You feel the pride and satisfaction of both being a confident person and of enjoying the things that happen to you as a result of your confidence. You visualize everything that would, or could, happen to you and live as if it really **is** happening to you.

Here's how to go about successful visualization:

FIRST: Decide what you want to do: pass an exam, get a promotion, meet someone new, make lots of money, be more confident, win the squash game.

SECOND: Relax. Spend several minutes unwinding so that you are comfortable in body and mind.

THIRD: Spend 5-10 minutes visualizing the reality you want.

Linger on thoughts of doing and having the thing you want now, not as some future reality that **might** happen or **could** happen. Live in your mind as if it's really happening to you. Create little inner film clips or videos. See yourself doing the thing you want. On one level, you know it's not yet happening to you; it's not yet real. It's still just a visualization, a mental picture. But the mental picture we indulge in, the one we regularly think about, becomes a blueprint for our goals, a mold into which we pour our energy.

Build whatever characteristics are necessary in your visualization.If talent, courage, determination, or persistence are vital parts of the picture, include them.Sometimes you will see clear, sharp images as if you are watching yourself featured in a movie, accomplishing your goal. Other times, you just sort of "think about" your goals in a general way; all this is fine. You can alternate between precise and free-flowing visualization, doing a few minutes of each, or concentrate on whatever technique feels most comfortable.

PRECISE VISUALIZATION: Put the exact pictures and scenes you want in your mind. Follow the pre-set script you have created and run it through your mind a number of times.

FREE-FLOWING VISUALIZATION: Allow images and thoughts to come and go without choosing them directly, **as long as they show a positive outcome of your goal.**

Practice both methods and remember the key here is **practice.** Most people find that they have difficulty in the beginning stages of visualization. Their mind won't co-operate and picture the desired scenes. Don't worry if this happens, the picture doesn't have to be complete and perfect. If you commit yourself to a program of regular visualization, you will be surprised at how your mind will gradually begin to think the thoughts and scenes you choose for it.

I should mention at this point, that visualizing something once or twice is of little effect. Results come when the image is imprinted again and again and **again** for a period of weeks or months until your goal has been achieved. Don't try to measure success after only one or two attempts.

If doubts or contradictory thoughts arise, and occasionally they will, just ignore them. Don't try to resist them or fight them, simply let those thoughts come and go in your consciousness without much notice. Just keep repeating your visualization and everything will quite naturally look after itself.

Two conditions to successful visualization:

(1) Always visualize your goal as if it's actually happening to you right now. Make it real in your mind; make it detailed. Enter the role and become it in your mind.

(2) Visualize your goal at least once a day, each and every day. There is power in repetition.

Any thought put into your mind, and nourished regularly, will produce results in your life

Let me share with you a recent University of Illinois experiment. A group of student basketball players was divided into three groups, tested for their ability to score baskets, and each group's results were recorded. The first group was then directed to come into the gym every day for a month to practice shooting, the second group was told to engage in no practice at all, and the third group was instructed to engage in a very different sort of practice. They didn't step foot in the gym, but instead, stayed in their dorms mentally imagining themselves there practicing. For half an hour each day they "saw" themselves throwing the ball and scoring baskets and improving dramatically. They continued this inner "practice" every day. After a month, the three groups were tested again.

The first group (those who practiced shooting every day) showed a 26% improvement in their scores. The second group (those who did no practice) showed no improvement. And the third group - who, remember, had practiced only in their minds - improved equally as much as the group that had practiced for real!

Such creative visualization is powerful, but it's far from magic. It involves working with natural laws and energies, and in being creative in directing your own innate power.

Properly directed, your imagination is one of the most dynamic faculties that you possess. Begin using this technique right away. You don't need to concern yourself with the specifics of how things will unfold. **Trust the process.** Supply follows demand and you will be led to do the right thing at the right time. You can be sure the ways and means will make themselves known to you for nature always creates the opportunities needed to fulfill the demands put upon her.

It's natural to want all the answers before we're willing to risk any legwork. We'd all love to see the steps and know all the details of everything that will happen to us. But you rarely get to see those details and steps at the beginning; and very often things unfold in the most unexpected ways.

Actress Carol Burnett was born in Los Angeles and raised by her grandmother. They scraped by on welfare and were so poor her grandmother collected toilet paper from public washrooms. There certainly was not enough money to send the talented youngster to U.C.L.A., which was her dream. She, however, knew she was going. "I never thought about the possibility of not going. I would imagine myself taking the classes, being on the campus, learning everything I wanted to learn. Every day I would think about it. Even though there didn't seem any way I could go, I knew I would."

So how did she get the money?

"One day in my final year of high school I went to the mailbox to check the mail. There was an envelope made out to me. It had a stamp on it, but it wasn't post marked. It hadn't been mailed, it had been hand delivered by someone. I opened the envelope and in it was the exact amount of my first year's tuition. No note. No explanation. Just the money. I still, to this day, don't know who sent it."

Opportunities open up when you open up your thoughts!

Now I am not saying that if you visualize it, someone will come up with an envelope and give you the exact money you want, the way it happened to Carol Burnett. But I do promise you that situations and opportunities will come your way that will lead you to your goal - you can count on it. Your thoughts are more powerful than you suspect, and any image held in the mind is a force that will eventually produce an effect.

It is not futuristic science fiction that we possess this ability, it already exists within us as a practical tool we can use any time we choose.

4.

Seeding

When an object or purpose is clearly held in thought, its precipitation, in tangible and visible form, is merely a question of time. The vision always precedes and itself determines the realization.

Lillian Whiting

I F visualization is creating visual scenes or pictures in your own movie, then seeding is like adding the sound track, only instead of words, you are adding the **feelings** that accompany the pictures.

For example, let's say you have an important presentation to make to your company. Your supervisors and bosses will all be present. If you do well there is an excellent chance you'll get a promotion as a result. The presentation is very important to your career. You decide to use the seeding technique, spending 5-10 minutes seeding the thought and feeling that you've just given the presentation and it was a huge success. Everyone was impressed. The interview is all over and you did it! - you pulled off a fabulous presentation.

Unlike visualization, in seeding you are primarily concerned with the "feeling" of whatever it is you are visualizing. Here is where your imagination comes into play. Imagine what it would be like to have delivered the "perfect" presentation. Would you be: Excited? Elated? Overjoyed? Relieved? Thrilled? Whatever your personal reaction, feel it in your guts and make those physical feelings a part of you. Live in the certainty that you already have the thing that you want. Don't wish, wonder, worry, or hope that it will go well. Claim it in your mind as an already existing fact. Replace "It's going to go well," with "It has gone well." It's all over and you did it, so enjoy the feeling of excitement, the sense of accomplishment, and the thrill of pulling it off! Congratulate yourself. Shout for joy. Leap up and down if you like. Exalt and vibrate again and again with the feeling of having already accomplished your goal.

Again, in seeding, you are not primarily interested in the mental pictures of how you'll achieve your goal, though these pictures will quite naturally flow into your mind. You can use visualization to help you get "the feeling", but it's not the visual, but the physical, sensation of accomplishment you're after: the flushed cheeks, the pounding heart, the sweaty palms.

In the Bible, Jesus's disciples ask him to teach them how to pray. (You may or may not believe the teachings of the Bible, however, it does contain some very powerful mind power techniques.) Jesus replies, "Whatsoever things ye pray for and ask for believing that ye have received, ye shall receive them." Notice he says that you must believe you **have** received them - not that you **will** receive them, but that you **have** received them - before you **will** receive them. This is more than just hoping or wishing, this is claiming what you want in the inner world, the world of thought and creative energy, and is a very powerful process as any person adept in working mind power will attest.

Let me share with you a story that happened to two very good friends of mine, Bill and Janet Henderson. The Hendersons were moving to Vancouver from a rural area, and they wanted to buy a house roomy and gracious enough to accommodate their growing family. Of course, houses are much more expensive in the city and they were a large family needing a large house. They also had very specific needs: not only did they want a large house, they wanted a large yard with lots of trees, and all at a price within their budget. Everyone told them they would never find anything like that for the price they wanted to pay, but they knew better. Bill had already practiced mind power techniques both in his job and in his relationship with his family, and knew they worked, so he enlisted Janet and together they worked as a team, visualizing and seeding for the house.

Two months later, they called me and asked me to come see their new home. We walked around their spacious yard as tranquil with its trees, shrubs, and flowers as if they had taken a piece of the country and brought it with them. Once inside, they gave me the full tour. It was a large house with enough bedrooms to give all the children their own rooms, and there was a den, and a recreation room - all for the price they had wanted to pay!

"That's fabulous!" I said, "Aren't you surprised you found it?"

Bill's answer showed such an enlightened understanding of the powers of the mind that I've never forgotten it. "No," he said. "We're not surprised at all. We had already taken possession of the house two months ago in our minds."

He said it with such confidence. After all, this was only the manifestation of something he had been claiming as his for two months. He and Janet had claimed the house in their inner world; they had taken possession of it already. Those are strong words. Strong vibrations. Powerful faith. They weren't hoping or wishing or wondering when and where they would find their dream house. They just worked regularly with the "feeling" that a house which would meet their needs would be theirs. They "took possession of it in their minds." Not this specific house, for until it came their way they had no idea that it even existed. But they did know what they wanted and needed and this is what they seeded every day until it became their reality.

Today, the Hendersons not only use seeding and other mind power techniques in their own lives, they are teaching their children the same principles so they, too, can have rich and rewarding lives. What greater gift could a parent give to their children than an understanding of their own natural powers?

We all have this power. Our thoughts create our reality, and seeding is merely working with the thought that you already have the thing you want.

It is repetition and consistency that separate seeding from idle daydreaming. In seeding, you don't live an illusion. You don't walk around every day with your head in the clouds believing you possess something you don't. Seeding is a mind power exercise that takes five minutes a day, a five minute burst of energy that you create for yourself regularly, each and every day, without fail. The importance of repetition cannot be overemphasized. As with all mind power techniques, practicing sporadically here and there is useless and will have little effect. Set yourself up a regular program and keep to it. Regularly seed the feeling that you already have whatever it is you want. It's yours. Live it. Vibrate it. Exalt and thrill with it. Claim it, absolutely, as yours. Take possession of it in the inner world.

Two conditions to successful seeding:

(1) Always seed with the feeling that you have the thing you want, that you have already achieved it.

(2) Seed regularly, each and every day, for at least five minutes. It is infinitely better to practice a few minutes every day than to do it for an hour once a week.

5.

Affirmations

The possibilities of thought training are infinite, its consequences eternal, and yet few take the pains to direct their thinking into channels that will do them good, but instead leave all to chance.

Marden

AFFIRMATIONS are probably the easiest and simplest technique we know to influence and affect the conscious mind. They have been used for centuries throughout the world in such spiritual and magical practices as prayers and mantras to replace negative thoughts with more positive ones. Now they are being used by people from all walks of life to close business deals, heal ailments, meet people, win tournaments, and in countless other applications.

Affirmations are simple statements repeated to yourself silently or aloud, whatever feels most comfortable and practical to you at the time. You can do them anywhere: in your car while you're driving, sitting in a waiting room waiting for an appointment, lying in bed before you go to sleep. You decide upon a statement that represents what you want to have happen to you, and you repeat it to yourself over and over again.

For example, let's say you're in a situation that usually upsets you and makes you tense when you'd prefer to be relaxed and calm. This is the perfect time to use an affirmation. Quietly repeat to yourself, "I feel calm and relaxed. I feel calm and relaxed. I feel calm and relaxed." Don't try forcing yourself to **feel** calm and relaxed, just keep repeating the statement to yourself for a couple of minutes. Likewise, if you have a big meeting coming up and you want it to go well, begin affirming to yourself beforehand, "It's going to be a great meeting. It's going to be a great meeting. It's going to be a great meeting."

What are you doing when you do affirmations?

When you are doing affirmations you are influencing the thoughts that go through your mind. Your mind can hold only one thought at a time so an affirmation works by "filling" your mind with thoughts that support your goal. The words suggest to the mind what it should be thinking. If you're affirming to yourself, "It's going to be a great meeting," your mind will quite naturally begin thinking thoughts about it being a great meeting. Your mind effortlessly picks up the implications and message of your affirmation. This simple technique can be very effective in helping you get the results you want.

Make whatever you want to see happen into an appropriate affirmation, and use it regularly. One successful salesman I know begins each day with the affirmation, "Lots of sales, lots of smiles," and he repeats this to himself for several minutes in the morning and several times throughout the day.

Things to remember when you are doing affirmations

(1) You don't necessarily have to believe them! In fact, anyone who's ever been unsuccessful in using affirmations has probably been trying to force themselves to do just that. This mistake can actually nullify the effects from the affirmation. Don't worry about believing, just keep repeating. If you do believe what you are affirming, great! If you don't believe it, that's fine, too. It doesn't matter. The conscious mind will quite naturally pick up the content of whatever you are affirming and it will seep into your consciousness. You don't have to force anything.

(2) Always affirm in the positive. Make a positive statement, not a negative one. For example, if you want to see a meeting go well, you wouldn't say, "I'm not going to blow this meeting." If you want to be calm and relaxed you wouldn't affirm, "I'm not going to be uptight." For some reason the mind doesn't pick up the "not" and you find yourself programming "blow the meeting" or "uptight." The mind will focus on these self-destructive images and not on what you want.

(3) Keep your affirmation short. An affirmation should

be like a mantra: short and simple, easy to say, and easy to repeat. I like to keep my affirmations to ten words or less. Sometimes even two words can be very effective: "Tremendous success," or "record sales."

I have had people show me affirmations that were half a page long. There's no way you can say an affirmation that long repeatedly. Even two sentences is too long. Repetition is what will imprint your affirmation into your consciousness, so the shorter the better. I repeat: make it short, make it rhythmic, make it easy to say.

Be careful that you don't use affirmations against yourself without realizing it.

"I'll never get it done,"

"I'll never do it,"

"It's impossible,"

"I'm blowing it,"

"I'm a disaster at relationships,"

"I'm bound to make a mistake,"

"I'm always losing,"

are all affirmations that you can find yourself repeating to yourself without even realizing it. Watch out for them.

Let me share with you an experience that happened to me on a lecture tour of Australia and New Zealand. Halfway through the tour, I looked at my schedule for the following months and couldn't believe my eyes. I was being routed from one city to another with hardly any breaks and was even expected to be in two different cities on the same day! I began thinking that the upcoming month would be an impossible, stress-filled pressure cooker and that's what I actually started telling myself - "This is going to be a pressure cooker." For two or three days I felt increasingly tense and uptight in anticipation of the dreadful next leg of the tour. I cursed the person who had set this ridiculous schedule for me.

Then I caught myself. I had to laugh. Here I was teaching mind power, and I'd unwittingly fallen into a trap of my own making. Nice affirmation, "I'm in a pressure cooker!" So I made myself a new affirmation consisting of just four words: **Organized, Relaxed, and Fun**, and I repeated this to myself for several minutes. The next morning I began the day with the same affirmation and I repeated it whenever I started thinking about my hectic schedule. Within a few days I began thinking that as long as I was organized and relaxed, the marathon pace might be fun. What was I getting all upset about?

In the end, those four words made all the difference. My schedule didn't change, but my attitude towards it did. The tour that I had almost made into a pressure cooker for myself turned out to be a breeze. I was organized, relaxed and had fun rushing about to meet the challenge, once I changed from a negative to a positive affirmation.

You can create affirmations and use them through your day to help you accomplish the things you want.

They are easy to say and can be done anywhere - in the bank queue, in the waiting room, or when stuck in traffic. You don't have to believe them. You don't have to do them with the sensation that you "have it." All you have to do is repeat them! I'd suggest starting first thing in the morning because that crucial first half-hour sets the tone for the rest of your whole day. As little as two or three minutes of practice will soon produce a noticeable effect.

"Every day in every way, it's getting better and better."

The name Emile Coue may not be a household word today, but at the turn of the century, this pioneer in affirmation technique was curing illnesses and teaching his discoveries in clinics all over Europe and North America. He caused quite a sensation in his day and his work is still talked about today, decades after his death. Coue found that his patients recovered much better, and more quickly, if they repeated a simple affirmation every morning upon rising and every evening before going to sleep. The affirmation he taught them was, "Every day in every way I'm getting better and better." Two minutes in the morning. Two minutes in the evening. That's all. The effect was so dramatic that he wrote several books on the subject of self-suggestion and taught people around the world the curative properties of the mind when directed towards recovery. Coue's affirmation focused the patient's mind on every day, in every way, getting better and better. Emile Coue is credited with the documented cures of thousands of people with this method.

Closer to our own time, singer-songwriter John Lennon will always be remembered for his music, his humanitarian beliefs, and his wonderful openness. Lennon made no secret of his interest in magic and the powers of the mind, and his songs reflect this interest. Listen to his lyrics for the song "Mind Games":

We're playing our mind games . . .
Creating the future, out of the now . . .

Lennon knew and used both visualization and affirmations. "Me mind is what makes it all happen," he liked to say, and in "Beautiful Boy," which he wrote for his son Sean, he actually sings, "Before you go to sleep - say this little prayer - "Every day in every way, it's getting better and better." He, like Coue and so many other great men and women before him, found his way to this eternal truth.

John Lennon's songs beckoned us to believe in ourselves and to believe in our power and our ability. "Who do you think you are?" he sang, "A superstar? Well, right you are!"

6.   Acknowledging

"Nothing succeeds like success."

MOST of us are quicker to see our own failures and shortcomings than we are to acknowledge our achievements and successes. When we accomplish something we feel good about it for a few days or weeks, but then we move on to new goals and new desires. All too quickly we leave behind the good feelings of accomplishment; we forget that we have even achieved them. Our new desires and wants become our focus and we let go of the success vibration that was created from our past achievements. This is a complete waste of powerful success energy. If we focus only on the not yet attained, we unconsciously feed the mind the idea that we are lacking. We could re-use success energies from past achievements again and again, with very positive results, but unfortunately, we rarely do so.

In Perth, Australia, a woman once came up to me after one of my lectures and asked, "John, do you think I could ever achieve my goals?" I asked her to describe them. Her first goal was to live in a beautiful house, her second goal was to fly back to England to see parents and relatives she hadn't seen in 14 years, and her third goal was to have a meaningful relationship with someone special. As she was a single mother with three children and lived on very slender means, these goals seemed impossible to her at the time. From my seminars, however, she hoped to learn powerful new ways to create her own reality.

I left Perth and didn't really think of the woman again until about a year later. Two months before I was to fly back I received a phone call from her.

"John," she said, all excited, "You'll never guess what happened! I now live in a new house with a swimming pool and a fabulous yard and view." I told her I was very happy for her, but she wasn't finished. "Not only that, but I was in England for three weeks and saw my family. And..." you could tell she was leaving the best for last, "I'm in the most fabulous relationship. I'm in love, really in love!"

Needless to say, I looked forward to seeing her again. She met me at the airport and as we were driving to the hotel she said to me, "John, why don't mind power work for me?"

I looked at her incredulously.

"Why doesn't mind power work for me?" she repeated. I had to ask her to pull over to the side of the road. I couldn't believe I was hearing this.

I said, "Listen, correct me if I'm wrong, but aren't you the woman who one year ago wanted to live in a nice house, travel to England, and have a meaningful relationship? Wasn't that you?"

She looked at me in embarrassment. "Oh," she said "I forgot about that!"

Forgot about that! How could anyone forget about it? Well, it's easy. We do it all the time. She had achieved her previous goals and now was working on new and different ones. Because she hadn't yet realized her new goals she was sincerely wondering why mind power weren't working for her. She had totally forgotten and taken for granted her most recent successful achievements. Her mind had moved on to new things.

We focus on what we want to achieve, totally forgetting to acknowledge what we **have** achieved. Why concern yourself with what you're not? We all have areas where we've failed, where we feel we don't measure up. Learn to pat yourself on the back for your present or past victories, no matter how small. Look for anything that makes you feel strong, victorious, successful, and good about yourself. Acknowledge anything and everything, small and large, and use it to create a vibration of success and achievement "in the now" which will aid you in attracting further success.

Acknowledgement is especially effective when

you are trying to achieve new goals. For example, let's say you're a young filmmaker trying to break into the big time by getting a major production company to back you. Using the acknowledging technique, you could look for areas that make you feel confident in your capabilities as a film maker. You might focus your thoughts on some of the short films you've made in the past and feel good about them. You might recall certain scenes that the critics said either worked well or showed real promise. Focus on these scenes and remind yourself that you also have a good eye for detail. Acknowledge all the hard work you've put into learning your craft. Recall all the compliments and praise people have given you about your work, and recognize all the skills you've developed over the last few years and the progress you've made.

Search, and I emphasize the word "search", for things to acknowledge. Don't just acknowledge the obvious; acknowledge everything. Don't feel silly or think it doesn't matter. Your positive qualities are just as real as the negative ones. Go ahead and feel proud. Feel great. Feel successful. Let your mind linger for several minutes on the success you already are.

This technique can be applied to any goal, not just in specific areas, but in a general way, as well. Take 10 minutes out right now and write down every strong point you can come up with in any area of your life, past or present.

Examples:

I dress well.

I'm good at my job.

I'm very creative.

I know a lot about ____.

I'm a good conversationalist.

I'm generous.

I'm a good painter.

I have a positive attitude.

I'm a safe driver.

I'm fun to be with.

Don't stop now. Your positive qualities are endless!

People like me.

I work hard.

I enjoy life.

I'm a loving partner.

I'm a conscientious parent.

I support my family and friends.

I've just completed making my acknowledging list.

Make a general list and make it **long.** List at least 20 items. Don't be timid and reserved about it - put it all down in black and white so you can see, in a concrete way, how many reasons you have to feel good about yourself. That's the purpose of this exercise, to make you realize you have lots of reasons to be proud of yourself. These good feelings create the success vibration that will form the foundation for your future success.

You can employ a similar approach when you are attempting to achieve any goal. Make a list of at least ten things about yourself which you can acknowledge that will support you in your attempt to achieve that goal. In trying to get a job as a sales manager, for example, you could make a list acknowledging the qualities that would make you a success at the job and, thus, the best candidate for the position.

Your list might look something like this:

I'm great with people.

I'm a good communicator.

People like me.

I work well with people.

I'm a born salesman.

I've done well in all my previous jobs.

I can motivate people.

I've been a successful sales manager before.

I'm talented.

I look and dress well.

I'm organized.

I work hard.

I achieve my goals.

If you hadn't made your list, you might have gone into the interview just **hoping** they'd give you the job. This way you go in certain you are qualified for the job.

"Nothing succeeds like success," and you **have** already succeeded in numerous areas. The more you vibrate this, the more success energy you attract from the environment. So make your lists. Feed your mind. Work with energy. Get involved in your life. Never stop acknowledging yourself. Neve stop believing in yourself. Don't wait for things to happen - begin creating, as John Lennon said, "the future out of the now."

Acknowledge. Acknowledge. Acknowledge.

Consciousness creates reality

and

you create consciousness

7. Beliefs and Imprinting

All truly wise thoughts have been thought already thousands of times; but to make them truly ours we must think them over again honestly, till they take root in our personal experience.

Goethe

THERE is no area of our life in which we don't have a set of beliefs and assumptions, some of which we accepted way back in early childhood and have defended ever since. Once acquired, we rarely question these beliefs. We naturally assume they are all true; why else would we have them? If we think it's hard to make money, it's because it **is** hard to make money. If we feel we are worthless, it's because we **are** worthless. If we know there are no opportunities for us, it's because there **are no** opportunities. We will doubt and scrutinize almost all aspects of our life but our beliefs are always the last to be challenged.

What you believe is what you get.

Most of us have unwittingly used our beliefs

against ourselves many times. If you look at any of your problem areas you'll probably find they are rooted in faulty and limited beliefs, so if you are having problems with your relationship, examine your beliefs about relationships. All your beliefs. Likewise, if you are having problems with health, look at your beliefs about health; if you are having financial problems, look closely at your beliefs about money.

After one of my lectures, a soft-spoken man in his mid-thirties confided to me that he had difficulties in making money. He always had just enough to support himself and his family, but never enough to save and get ahead. "I'll never have enough money," he shrugged, "It's impossible to get ahead."

These two negative beliefs, "I'll never have enough money" and "It's impossible to get ahead," lodged deep in his subconscious mind, were continuously at work coloring this man's reality. I suggested to him that these might not be the only limiting beliefs he held about money for, in my experience, most limiting beliefs drag a host of undesirable relatives along with them.

I asked him to write down all his beliefs about money and success. The resulting list was quite revealing. It included such commonly held beliefs as: "If I accept money from someone then they will go without," "There are no good opportunities left to make money," "Money is hard to make," "Successful people are selfish and I don't want to be selfish," and "I would have to give up too much to become successful." Quite a self-limiting and self-defeating list!

No wonder this man couldn't get ahead financially - he was at war with his own subconscious which kept telling him he would have to become selfish, take from others, and give up "too much" in order to make more money.

At another of my lectures, a woman who had suffered constant poor health found, upon examining her beliefs, that she was telling herself: "Everyone gets sick," "There is so much disease around," "I catch everything," "My body is fragile," and "Disease is much more powerful than health." Luckily, she was able to turn her health around in time, by adopting new life-strengthening beliefs.

What is in your subconscious mind is of immense concern to you. If your subconscious mind has picked up worry, negativity or limiting suggestions, it will accept them as true and will work with that belief day and night bringing about the corresponding situations. If it believes in poverty, failure, and trouble, then it will endeavour in a thousand different ways to manifest those realities. What is contained in your subconscious mind and the experiences you encounter in your life are directly connected to one another.

Have you swallowed any snakes?

There's an old Zen parable about a foolish peasant who was sent to visit his master's house. The master brought him into the study and offered him some soup, but just as the peasant was about to drink it, he noticed a small snake in his bowl. Not wanting to offend his master he drank it anyway, and within a few days fell so ill that he was brought back to the house.

The master again took him into his study and prepared some medicine which he gave to the peasant in a small bowl. Just as the peasant was about to drink the medicine, he noticed another snake in the bowl. This time he pointed it out and loudly complained that this was the reason he was sick in the first place. Roaring with laughter, the master pointed to the ceiling from which hung a large bow. "It is the reflection of the bow you are seeing," he said. "There is no snake at all."

The peasant looked again and, sure enough, there was no snake in his bowl, only a reflection. He left the house without taking the medicine and regained his health within the day.

We have accepted limitations about ourselves and our world that are holding us back. We have swallowed imaginary mental snakes by accepting limitations and believing they are true. And they are always true . . . until we find out otherwise.

Once your subconscious mind has accepted a belief or idea, whether true or not, it will continually feed you thoughts to support that belief. Let's say you unconsciously believe that it is hard to establish a loving relationship. This belief, repeated to yourself, soon becomes imprinted on the subconscious mind. Once imprinted, it will feed your mind with thoughts such as "I'll never meet someone I like," "It's impossible to meet a good partner," "Relationships never work," and so on.

When you meet someone special your thoughts become "He's probably not that nice," "Why bother trying, it won't work," or "She'd never be interested in me." Furthermore, your mind, convinced that "It's hard to have a good relationship," will magnify any incidents that support this belief and will ignore or dismiss incidents which indicate the opposite. Our mind will distort our perception of reality to make it conform to our beliefs.

Think you are worthless? Or that it's hard to make money? Believe you are susceptible to poor health? Your mind will find irrefutable evidence to support those beliefs and will work overtime to manifest those realities.

On the other hand, if you believe that you are a winner, or that there's money to be made everywhere - if you believe in your own vibrant health - you'll find yourself surrounded by equally strong evidence supporting **those** beliefs.

Choose your beliefs wisely.

In almost all problem areas of your life, **you** are the problem and **you** are the solution. It may not seem that way, but you are encountering your resistance, not from outside sources, but from inside yourself - from your beliefs. New beliefs when accepted by our subconscious mind will open up whole new realities.

For example, let's say you believe that "it's hard to make friends." Holding this belief now excuses you from making friends: it's not your fault - it's hard! It's only logical and understandable that you don't make friends. Your belief deludes you into believing that your lack of friends has nothing to do with **you**.

If you change your belief to "it's easy to make friends" your telephone may not suddenly start ringing off the hook with dinner invitations, in fact, you may not make even a few friends, but you will have changed your focus. Suddenly the problem isn't out there: the problem is with you. Once you take responsibility for your reality, you can examine what you need to change in yourself and sometimes just that change of attitude will open up numerous possibilities.

As you continue to believe that "it's easy to make friends" you will find plenty of evidence to support this belief and will make whatever changes in yourself are necessary to take advantage of this newly emerging reality.

Challenge yourself to greatness!

Challenge yourself to create new, more supportive beliefs even if on the surface you don't believe them. Remind yourself that you can voluntarily plant in your subconscious mind any thought, idea, or belief you desire and your mind will accept it provided it is introduced with feeling and reinforced through repetition.

The subconscious mind is a creature of habit. If you have allowed limiting concepts to root there you can crowd them out by constructing new and more supportive beliefs and practicing them until the old ideas have been replaced by the new ones. The subconscious mind will not question these new beliefs; it accepts any thought repeatedly dwelt upon.

Do a mental house cleaning. Change the furniture and paint the walls. It's time to toss out all those old limiting, self defeating beliefs, however cherished, and replace them.

Check the following list carefully to see if you are you in the habit of using even one of these sayings:

I can't do it.

I'll never get ahead.

There are no opportunities right now.

I've tried hundreds of times.

It doesn't matter what I do.

I don't care what happens.

It's hard to get ahead.

Something always goes wrong.

It won't last.

Life is hard.

You have to work hard for everything you achieve.

Nothing comes easy.

This is not the right time.

I don't know what to do.

If any of these sound familiar, begin immediately to imprint new, more supportive beliefs. Allowing ourselves to succeed means being willing to give up the excuses, the security, and the other "benefits" we have derived from failure. Millions of people are content to stay as they are and will make no attempt to change. They believe life is hopeless and difficult and have resigned themselves to this fate; nothing will shake them from it.

Explore your Possibilities

Step 1:

Pick an area of your life in which you are having difficulty - finances, relationships, sex, health, business, etc.

Write down all your beliefs about the area. Take your time and be honest. Don't write what you think you should feel or what looks good, write what you really feel deep down. When you have finished, examine the list and search for limiting beliefs. We are not interested in whether these beliefs are true or not, only in whether or not they're limiting.

This process, if done honestly, can be quite revealing in itself.

Step 2:

Beside each limiting belief write a newer, more supportive belief. For example:

Limited Beliefs:	*New Beliefs:*
There are no ways for me to make money	There are many undiscovered ways for me to make money

Limited Beliefs:	*New Beliefs:*
It is hard to meet people	It is easy to meet people
It's hard to make friends	It is easy to make friends
I'll never get ahead	I'm bound to succeed
I have no time to work on this project	There will be lots of time to work on this project

Using the imprinting technique which follows, impress these new beliefs into your subconscious mind. Stick to one or two new beliefs a month; don't try to do too much at one time. As the months roll by you will find you have a number of powerful new beliefs working for you.

Imprinting

The imprinting technique is simple: you've been using it almost since birth. You've used it to learn first your language, and then facts like the multiplication tables. You immediately know the answer to "6 x 6" or "8 x 7" because the answers have been imprinted in your mind through numerous exercises and repetition. Remember how many times you wrote and memorized your multiplication tables? You probably don't remember learning to read either, but you did so by the same method continually repeating words and phrases and correcting yourself, or being corrected when you mispronounced or misused them. Now you can speak your own language effortlessly, because it has been imprinted into your mind.

Like any other new information, ideas and beliefs must be imprinted in your mind before you can use them successfully and automatically. The thrill of a new idea cannot be sustained, for inspiration, however strong, soon fades and disappears. However motivated a person may be, if they are unable or unwilling to follow through on their initial enthusiasm, they will inevitably lapse back into their original position, their old ways.

When imprinting, use a combination of affirmations and contemplations. While repeating the idea to yourself, think about it. Make it real to yourself and ignore any contrary ideas. The new concept is still a tender shoot, nurture it through its first struggling stages. Be vigilant, for without care your unruly old ideas, like mental weeds, will take over and crowd it out.

There is a necessary germination period before any new idea or belief will take root and flourish in our consciousness. This takes time. It does not happen by whipping past a new belief once or twice, or even ten or twenty times. True imprinting requires one to three months before its effects are firmly fixed in the mind. That's thirty to ninety imprinting sessions of 5 - 10 minutes each day. Can you see why people who try to adopt a new belief by reading it once or twice are doomed to fail? "I've tried to believe it but I just can't," they say hopelessly. Yet how hard did they try?

You are trying to create new beliefs in your subconscious mind, and very often these new beliefs contradict the existing beliefs you now hold. It's simply not possible for your mind to incorporate any new belief unless you intend to imprint it daily for a month or two.

Why waste your time and disappoint yourself with half-hearted attempts? Every new belief needs time and attention to flourish, anything less will not succeed. Now repeat after me:

> Every new belief needs time and attention to flourish.

> Every new belief needs time and attention to flourish.

> Every new belief needs time and attention to flourish.

> Get the message?

8.

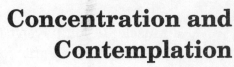

Concentration and Contemplation

> To fully understand a grand and
> beautiful thought requires, perhaps,
> as much time as to conceive it.
>
> ***Joubert***

MOST people have an erroneous idea of
what concentration is. They associate it
with hard work and sometimes painful
school memories. If, however, you've
ever lost yourself in the enjoyment of a movie or
concert, you've found that concentrating comes naturally when you are absorbed in something you enjoy.

In fact, deep concentration requires no superhu-
man effort on your part. Just the opposite is true
always, always, always "concentrate easy." Let
yourself become so engrossed in your subject that you
are conscious of nothing else. Think of a skillful actor:
his greatness lies in his ability to lose himself in the
portrayal of his character.

Developing your concentration is like developing

a muscle. If you haven't been to the gym for a while you'll find even a light workout tortureous. But if you continue working out every day, you will soon find you can do ever more sit-ups and lift even heavier weights with increasing ease.

It's the same with contemplation. Your mind is not used to disciplined thinking so your first few tries will not be nearly as effective as they will be after you have been mentally working out for a while. Be patient with yourself and give yourself time to develop these new skills.

Contemplation

Since it is through contemplation that we deepen our understanding, it should form an integral part of our training. With contemplation we break through the surface of things, to explore their deeper meaning and implications as have artists, mystics, and religious and spiritual leaders throughout the ages.

Without contemplation we fool ourselves into believing that because we can quote facts or make intellectual arguments about a subject we know everything there is to know about it. We may know something on a factual surface level but that doesn't mean we "know it," at all.

Consider the difference between a tomato picked while still small, hard and green, and one allowed to sunripen to its sweet, juicy fullness. You could say you know what a tomato tastes like after having eaten the green one and technically you would be right. After sampling that luscious ripe one, however, you'd immediately see how much you'd missed. Your awareness of the possibilities of "tomato" had broadened. You had tasted both stages and now knew the difference. Likewise, you could say you now understand how mind power work, and it is true that by reading this book you have received the basic information, but it is through daily practice that your comprehension will develop beyond the beginner's level. Your current understanding is like a tiny seed that will flower and bear fruit if you cultivate it through contemplation.

To practice contemplation

Pick a quotation, saying, theme, or parable - anything that inspires you. Using a watch or clock to time yourself, devote five minutes to concentrating on the material. Lose yourself in it, thinking deeply about it. Ask yourself questions such as: What does this mean? What are its implications? How do they affect me? Can I make this concept work for me?

When your mind wanders (and it will wander), gently but firmly bring it back to the subject of your reflections, and do not let any apparent failure or slow progress deter you from continuing with the exercise. Totally irrelevant thoughts are sure to drift into your mind in the middle of your practice. Memories of recent events, tasks waiting to be done, desires, worries, and fantasies will enter uninvited and try to hold the field of attention. As soon as you become aware that the intrusion is out of place, dismiss it and begin again at the point where you left off.

Your lazy mind is not used to being disciplined and directed in this way. It prefers to meander about thinking what it wants, when it wants. When the mind becomes bored with contemplation it will want to move on to something more interesting. Just keep bringing it back again and again to your central theme and press on with this inner inquiry moving from thought to thought in linked sequence.

"If you read a book a thousand times you are bound to understand it," says an old Chinese proverb. Likewise, if you pursue your contemplation for a period of weeks and months, not only will you deepen and enrich your understanding, but by disciplining and directing your mind you will naturally and effortlessly develop your powers of concentration.

Contemplate all aspects of your training until you understand it fully. It's a good idea to keep a pen and paper handy when contemplating so you can write down any new insights as they come to you.

Part Two

9.

Reality

Man has his future within him,
dynamically alive at this present
moment.

Abraham Maslow

WHAT is happening right now in your life
is not happening to you as a result of
chance. Your past consciousness, your
past thoughts, have helped to create it.
Your "now" has its causes and roots in your past
thinking.

Consider the following analogy: When you look up
into the sky and see the stars, what you are actually
seeing is the past because some of those stars may no
longer exist. This is possible because stars are hundreds and thousands of light years away, meaning that
it takes their light, travelling at 186,000 miles a
second, hundreds or thousands of years to reach the
earth. Thus, the light we see from a star a hundred
light years away is actually light it emitted a hundred
years ago. That particular star could have exploded

and disintegrated 25 years ago, but we still see its light, and will continue to see its light, for another 75 years even though the star itself has long ceased to exist.

This analogy is crucial to keep in mind when using mind power techniques to change your reality for even when you change your thoughts, your new reality will not immediately follow. There will always be a certain time lag during which you will be in a position of developing a new consciousness, but still stuck with your old reality.

This "waiting for it to happen" period is critical because how you react during this waiting period will either quicken or hinder the new reality you are attempting to create. You may doubt things are changing. You may feel discouraged and wonder if you are wasting your time. Your mind will try and fool you by telling you nothing will happen - this won't work. These thoughts are natural; they happen to us all. Do not pay them any heed, just continue with your exercises, being patient and diligent in your efforts. It helps to remember that reality is a process - a continuous happening - and not something fixed and rigid.

Everything in existence is continually in the process of becoming something else. Your circumstances, too, are forever changing and becoming something else so how could your new thoughts, if persisted in, do anything but bring you a new reality? Think about it.

Relax and enjoy your exercises, ignoring any negative thoughts. Your life will change naturally and effortlessly. You don't have to force it.

Keep these points in mind:

(1) Be conscious of what you are doing. You are creating your future experiences with your "now" thoughts.

(2) Change your reaction to any undesirable conditions in your life. If you are struggling in your career, without a relationship, sick, unemployed, or nothing seems to be working for you, the first thing you must do is accept the situation. Don't try to pretend it isn't happening. It is. Don't waste time feeling sorry for yourself or fighting it; work through it with mind power. How you decide to think and react during this period determines what is going to happen to you.

(3) Establish a daily inner "creating" period for yourself free from everyday demands and distractions. It is this inner creating period that gives you power.

I once called a company to get some important information which I needed for my business. The woman I spoke to asked me to call back in half an hour explaining "I'm sorry. We can't get into our computer right now, it's running a program." I put down the receiver and thought to myself, "That's exactly how we practice mind power. When we run a mental program we close off our mind to all outer distractions and run our program over and over again in our mind."

Change is a cumulative process

Imagine you have an eye dropper full of red dye and every day you squeezed one drop of dye into a large bowl of water. At first, you would see no effect because the dye would quickly disappear and be absorbed. If, however, you continued to add a drop every day, the water would gradually turn from clear to pale pink, to deep rose, and finally to brilliant red.

In creating a new reality for yourself your "ink dropper" is that daily creating period during which you detach yourself from your worries, your difficulties, and your "now" reality. This period can be anything from five minutes to thirty minutes, so long as you observe it every day. By regularly and diligently applying the techniques you have learned, an ever increasing effect is seen. Those who practice half-heartedly soon fall by the wayside, but nothing is beyond the reach of those who have vision, understanding, and commitment.

Will you dare to believe in your vision as being stronger and more potent than present circumstances?

Are you willing to infuse yourself daily, without fail, with thoughts of your desired reality?

Will you persevere, trusting in your daily practice and refusing to believe otherwise, even in the face of seemingly unchanged or contradictory conditions?

If you can, then you shall have whatever you desire. You will step forward boldly into the world and the world will give you whatever you ask.

10.   Intuition

We lie in the lap of immense intelligence.
> *Emerson*

Ask and ye shall receive. Knock and the door will be opened.
> *Matthew 7:7*

ALL great achievers, whether they be businessmen, athletes, artists, or statesmen, trust and use their intuition. The ability to come up with inspired ideas and make astute decisions is the mark of one who has cultivated his inner self.

I once had a chance meeting with one of Australia's richest and boldest entrepreneurs. We were in a Perth hotel lobby one evening about an hour before I was due to speak. I recognized him from his pictures in various newspapers and magazines, so I approached him and introduced myself. I had read in a magazine article that he believed strongly in intuition, and I asked him if that was true. "Intuition plays a major role in everything I do," he confirmed. "I can't think of one major venture that I have entered upon without first checking with my intuition."

This man is not alone: Mozart claimed he received his inspiration from within; Socrates said he was guided by his inner voice. Einstein, Edison, Marconi, Henry Ford, Luther Burbank, Madame Currie, Nobel laureates by the bundle, J.J. Thompson, Alexis Carrel, Max Planck - the list goes on and on of great men and women who have attributed their success directly to their intuition.

Henry Mintzberg, in the Harvard Business Review, describes a study he did on high ranking corporate executives in which he found that they were "constantly relying on hunches to cope with problems too complex for rational thinking." He concluded: "Success does not lie in that narrow-minded concept called 'rationality'; it lies in a blend of clear headed logic and powerful intuition."

Conrad Hilton tells the story of how he submitted a bid for $165,000 for a piece of property he wished to purchase for a hotel. When he awoke the following morning the number 180,000 was nagging him. "Connie" is well known for following his hunches, which he calls his "invisible counselors," so he changed his bid. He did secure the property, which eventually sold for over 2 million dollars, for $180,000 because the next highest bid was $179,000.

Ray Kroc bought MacDonalds against the advice of his lawyers and accountants because "I felt it in my funny bone that it was a sure thing." MacDonalds is now a very sure thing - it's the most successful franchise operation in the world - and Kroc's decision to buy "a few hamburger stands" has made him a multi-millionaire hundreds of times over.

Paying attention to intuition enables an individual to make better decisions, to come up with more creative ideas and deeper insights, and to find the smoothest, most direct route from desire to fulfillment. Those people who always seem to be in the right place at the right time, and for whom good things happen with uncanny frequency, are not just lucky, they have developed an intuitive sense of what to do and when to do it. Their intuition allows them to go beyond the obvious to come up with fresh, innovative possibilities. It supplies them with all they need to know and instructs them on when and how to use that knowledge a most precious and valuable asset in life.

How does intuition work?

I spoke earlier of our minds as being bits of a greater hologram whose whole is contained in each and every one of its parts. Our subconscious mind is linked and connected to the entire system and thus has access to all the information contained within that system.

This is hardly a new revelation. Traditionally, in the study of magic, the occultist is taught early in his training that we are but a microcosm of the macrocosm - a little universe in miniature - and that all the power that exists outside of us exists inside of us, as well.

Twentieth century psychologist and philosopher

Carl Jung referred to the subconscious as "no mere depository of the past, but full of future psychic situations and ideas." This isn't at all far-fetched if you think of the universe as a vast pattern of energy with every event and every thought contributing to it. Your subconscious mind, as a part of the system, can draw upon any information or event it wishes. Your everyday conscious mind may know and understand only your own personal experiences and knowledge, but your subconscious mind can access anything in the system, past, present, and in some cases, even future.

Calling up solutions from the subconscious mind

Whenever you need an answer or solution from your subconscious, follow these three steps spending 3 to 4 minutes on each. The entire process should take approximately ten minutes.

STEP 1: The first step is to simply contemplate the fact that the right decisions, ideas, and solutions already exist and are waiting for you "now" in your subconscious mind. Your subconscious mind is a reservoir of all you could ever need or require. Answers and solutions exist in abundance, all there waiting for you. The pressure is off; relax in confidence that you contain a wealth of resources.

STEP 2: State clearly what you want from your subconscious mind and silently repeat to yourself instructions that you wish it to carry out. In practicing this step don't try to come up with answers or let yourself feel pressured or confused. Simply state what it is you require, repeating your request again and again. You will reach the subconscious mind by repeating your instructions.

STEP 3: Relax and fill your mind with faith and expectancy that the correct answer will come to you. Remember, faith and confidence are not only attitudes, but vibrations of energy. These vibrations will attract the appropriate solutions and answers just as a magnet attracts metal filings. A mind vibrating with belief that answers are coming to it naturally draws those answers. If you had the correct and perfect solution, imagine how you would feel: excited, overjoyed, relieved. Feel those sensations now. Let your mind play with this mood in a relaxed way. Drop off to sleep with the assurance that the answers are soon to be yours.

This entire process is best done each evening before you go to sleep. This twilight period between conscious and subconscious levels is the most opportune time to reach the subconscious.

Receiving the information

Sometimes the answer will come as a hunch or insight that pops into your mind when you least expect it, perhaps when you are driving your car or eating breakfast. Other times, it comes as the "still small voice within" during your silent, quiet periods.

Frequently, intuitive ideas come to us in dreams. Dr. Frederick Banting, the brilliant Canadian physician, discovered the basics of insulin in a dream which instructed him in exactly what steps to take to find the elusive formula. Elias Howe, the inventor of the sewing machine, laboured for years over its design, yet always remained one small detail from his goal. One night he dreamt he had been captured by savages who were pointing strange spears at him, and he noticed that at the tip of each spear was a hole. Howe awoke from his dream with the solution: put the hole at the tip of the needle! That simple change was the key that unlocked the invention of the sewing machine.

The methods the subconscious uses to bring you information will vary from one time to the next, but you will always know you are receiving intuitive information by the quality of the ideas and by the feelings they produce within you. The exhilaration, the certainty, and the overpowering sense that "this is it!" which accompany subconscious information will distinguish it from just another idea. Proficiency comes with practice so work with and trust your gut feelings.

Staying open to intuition

Certain attitudes and behavior will encourage intuition and these are worth cultivating. In many ways we tell the subconscious mind what we expect from it, and we usually get what we expect. Acceptance and confidence create receptivity. If you can learn to think of your intuition as a normal and valuable part of daily living, and issue an open invitation to come at any time, it will show up bearing gifts. "I can't solve that problem" or "I'll never find the answer" signal the intuition not to bother. Confident thoughts and the conviction that you deserve and expect not only **an** answer, but the **best** answer, stir intuition to positive action.

Don't be timid. Boldly tell your subconscious mind that its wisdom, knowledge, and power are guiding and instructing you.

Some affirmations you might want to try are:

I always make the right decisions.

My subconscious mind works for me day and night.

All answers exist "now" within me.

My subconscious mind is my partner in success.

This last affirmation is one I practice for a week or two whenever I want to prime my intuition. If you break this affirmation down, you will see that it contains three powerful keys:

(1) "My subconscious mind . . ." by affirming this you acknowledge to yourself that you do, indeed, have a subconscious mind. You are recognizing and accepting your "unseen partner" as real.

(2) ". . . is my partner." A partner is someone who works side by side with you to achieve a common goal.

Someone with whom you split the workload, each of you tackling different areas. Why not let your subconscious partner specialize in the area to which it is best suited - namely, supplying you with accurate information, ideas and answers? You are never alone, never without guidance, because you can always count on your subconscious mind. It supplies the ideas; you supply the action.

(3) ". . . in success." The word "success" is a powerful affirmation representing everything you want to see happen to you in business, in relationships, and in life. Just the act of repeating the affirmation sets vibrations of energy in motion that will greatly assist you in achieving your goal.

The quality of your life depends upon the quality of your thoughts and ideas. How many times have you fruitlessly searched your mind for solutions, going over the same information time and time again in the hope that you've missed something? The answers weren't there because by searching only your conscious mind you've greatly limited your possible solutions. You've put a blindfold on yourself and tied one hand behind your back. No wonder you are not succeeding to the degree you desire - it's in the treasure house of the subconscious mind that new ideas, answers, and solutions exist in abundance. Don't limit yourself. Dig into the rich trove of information and help yourself. Why use the same old tired, worn out ideas you've been hashing and rehashing for years? Why invest even more effort in ideas that aren't working? You need something new and dynamic that is full of life and spirit and originality. You need the perfect answers, the perfect solution, the perfect ideas, and they all exist "now" just below your conscious level of thinking. It's all right here, "now", inside you.

Once you recognize the omnipotent power that exists in the subconscious mind, you will never want for answers. You will merely adjust your consciousness and direct it to bring you the required information. As the Upanishads say, "All exists within."

Mind Power

86

11.

Self Image

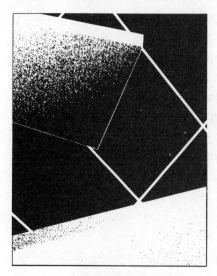

Something we were withholding
made us weak until we found
it was ourselves.
Robert Frost

WHILE most everyone would agree on the importance of a good, healthy self image, few people know how to acquire one or understand how they helped to form the one they now possess.

Our self image is exactly what it says: an image made up of ideas about ourselves that we have formed over the years. Once this image becomes imprinted on the subconscious mind and forms a structured pattern, it takes on a life of its own and we forget that it is something we have created, which can be changed and altered to better fit our present needs and requirements.

Let us look closer at how self image is formed. In childhood, when our "worth" was first established, we accepted all kinds of ideas about ourselves. If our parents were loving and supportive, we most likely feel relatively good about ourselves; if our parents abused, ridiculed, or belittled us, we may have a less positive self image. As we grew up and moved away from our parents out into the world of our peers and other adults, countless other experiences impressed themselves upon us. Unfortunately, if we have made a habit of dwelling over life's inevitable disappointments, we may have made them the central part of our overall image.

Building a strong self image

A car that is not maintained properly will inevitably become a wreck. A house that is not kept up will become rundown and dilapidated. Your self image, likewise, must be maintained if you want it to be strong and vibrant. It is through ignorance and neglect that a self image deteriorates. Take responsibility. Take care of your self image as you would take care of yourself.

Life is full of temporary disappointments, heartaches, failures, and problems, and if we are not careful these can easily drag us down. We need to regularly reinforce our self image in order to keep it healthy. We can do this by setting up a regular program to feed our mind with positive, uplifting, inspiring thoughts about ourselves. We can even cheat a little and include thoughts that aren't yet true. Remember, your subconscious mind will accept any thought about yourself that you regularly think, and that idea will eventually become part of your self image.

Three useful concepts can be imprinted which will immediately strengthen your self image:

(1) **You are unique.**

No one else has your thoughts, your ideas, or your ways of doing things. Most people think they are ordinary but don't **YOU** make that mistake. Don't just recognize your uniqueness, proclaim it through your actions and in your daily thinking. Feel good about being alive and being you. Carry yourself with the dignity you deserve and you put yourself at a very great advantage.

(2) **You can do anything.**

We forget that life affords us countless possibilities and choices and we too often become bogged down in our day to day routines, losing sight of what can be done if we but put our minds to it.

You can travel to any country.

You can learn any language.

You can start any business.

You can learn to play any musical instrument.

You can join any group.

You can learn any craft.

You can develop any trade.

You can change jobs.

You can begin any project.

You can think any thoughts.

What **can't** you do if you put your mind to it? You have programs already written into your vast computer mind that cover every possibility. I call them our holographic possibilities. A tomato seed has only one possibility and that is to be a tomato. A rose cannot do anything but become a rose. Its fate is locked into that one reality, but you have infinite potential. The seed of whatever you choose to be is contained within you.

(3) You have unlimited power.

Every day of your life, you wake up with limitless power at your disposal. The power I speak of is the ability to choose your thoughts. Nobody tells you what to think or how to think. You, and you alone, determine what you do with this power. You can create, build, and strengthen any area of your life.

You will become whatever you consistently think about yourself

Timid thoughts create a timid person.

Confident thoughts create a confident person.

Weak thoughts create a weak person.

Strong thoughts create a strong person.

Thoughts with purpose create a person with purpose.

Visionary thoughts create a visionary person.

Thoughts of helplessness create a helpless person.

Thoughts of self pity create a person filled with self pity.

Enthusiastic thoughts create an enthusiastic person.

Loving thoughts create a loving person.

Successful thoughts create a successful person.

YOU are responsible for your own self image and **YOU** are responsible for creating and maintaining it. Acknowledge yourself regularly. Visualize, seed, and affirm positive qualities for yourself.

Love yourself

Self love is very important - not an "I'm better than you are," but a nurturing feeling that "I'm O.K. as I am" - a realization that you don't have to be anything other than what you are. It is ironic that the moment you can accept yourself as you are, you can easily change yourself and become something different. So long as you dislike yourself it is difficult to change, for it is self acceptance at the deepest levels which frees us to move on. Take the pressure off. You don't have to be anybody other than yourself. Once you accept that, you can explore some of the other "selves" you might want to become.

Self confidence

Insist on self confidence. Settle for nothing less than a firm belief and conviction that you can, and will, succeed. If you have had an unfortunate childhood, put it behind you; you are here now and your future awaits. If you have failed previously, so what? The only thing that counts is what you now think and what you do with those thoughts. As your self image becomes stronger and more confident, life's situations will become easier, for as you change, so does everything around you. It is entirely in your hands.

12.

No Problems, Only Opportunities

The real alchemist is one who learns the secret of turning everyday situations into gold, who learns how to make every situation serve him.

John Kehoe

MOST of us dream of the day when we won't have any more problems, when everything will be resolved and our lives will be "complete." But problems are an important and valuable part of our lives, and instead of trying to eliminate them, we should strive to understand exactly what they really are.

Nothing happens by chance. We are a part of a universe that is forever giving us definite messages and signals, often in the form of problems. It is not an accident or coincidence that a particular problem is happening to you at any given point in your life; our difficulties are sign posts waiting to be read. Ask yourself: What is the problem I'm experiencing telling me about myself? What is it telling me about my thoughts? Beliefs? Actions? Choices? Lifestyle? **What is this problem trying to tell me?**

Look closely and see if you can find the real cause. If you feel sorry for yourself or helpless when a problem comes your way, you'll miss the important messages it brings you.

Become an alchemist

The medieval alchemist spent his lifetime trying to learn the secrets of turning ordinary base metals into gold. Much time and great fortunes were spent in this pursuit with little success because its practitioners were looking in the wrong direction. The real alchemist is one who learns the secret of turning everyday situations into gold, who learns how to make every situation serve him. Problems and difficulties can be used as a springboard to deeper insight and the real alchemist understands that there are no such things as problems, only opportunities.

No such things as problems, only opportunities

Once a person takes on this belief and works at finding the opportunities that are contained within each situation, the experiences that follow this simple change of attitude are quite startling.

Margaret Kelly, a Vancouver woman who had attended my Thought Dynamics seminars, found an opportunity to practice this principle one day at work. She was the director of a huge nursing home and, together with her two assistants, managed the day to day affairs of over a thousand patients. If even one of her assistants was off sick it created havoc, so you can imagine the "problem" she faced one day when both called in sick. She panicked until she remembered that "there are no such things as problems, there are only opportunities." Where is the opportunity here, Margaret wondered?

Margaret realized she was always working through her two assistants and didn't really know some of the staff they worked with. She told herself, "I'm going to use this as an opportunity to get to know these other people." She spent the day talking and working with employees with whom she normally had little contact. She listened to their concerns and to the difficulties they were having which, in turn, led to a whole new and more effective way of administering certain duties. As Margaret Kelly later told me, "The day turned out to be a wonderful opportunity and I accomplished so much."

I doubt Margaret Kelly would have been able to turn such a tense situation to her advantage as successfully as she did had she dwelt upon her so-called problem. It was changing her attitude from "I've got a huge problem" to "there are no such thing as problems, only opportunities" which had enabled her to try the new course of action which produced such rich results.

Nancy Spencer was facing the biggest problem of her life when I first met her. She had been deserted by her common law husband and left with three small children. She had no money, no working skills, and was desperate. It seemed like an insurmountable problem until Nancy began reminding herself that there are no such things as problems, there are only opportunities. But where? She searched for over a week before she finally found the opportunity she was looking for.

She realized, upon examining herself, that she had always been dependant upon someone - first her parents, and then her common law husband. She had allowed other people to tell her what to do because she had very low self-esteem. Now, in the depths of despair, in a seemingly hopeless situation, she made a promise to herself. Nancy resolved to rise up and become a confident and successful person for herself and her children. She would use this crisis as a springboard to become a strong and independent adult.

I was pleased I had the opportunity of teaching Nancy the concepts covered in this book for she was an avid student and worked regularly and persistently on her self image, her beliefs, and her goals. I watched her change before my very eyes and saw her progress from taking her first menial jobs to opening her own wholesale flower business. Today she is a happy, successful, self-confident woman married to a warm and sincere man. They share a wonderful life together - all because Nancy believed that there are no such thing as problems, there are only opportunities.

Become an alchemist in life and make every situation serve you. Remember that many times we reject or complain about events which, in retrospect, were necessary to our growth and development.

One of the great inventions of the 1950s came about when researcher Don Stookey accidently left some treated glass in the furnace so long it turned white. Undaunted, Stookey creatively turned that accident to his advantage by continuing to experiment with the new substance and, when he found it could withstand searing heat, further refining and marketing his mistake as "Corning Ware," a product now found in almost every home in North America.

Learn to see your stresses and struggles as challenges and opportunities, not liabilities or handicaps. Consider the story of entrepreneur Kathy Kolbe who was born dyslexic, unable to tell left from right or read the time on a clock without great difficulty. "My disability is one of the greatest advantages I have," she says, "It helped me become a student of the thinking process."

In 1979 Kolbe took $500.00 of her savings and launched a firm called Resources for the Gifted. She compiled a catalogue of available resources for intellectually gifted children and sent it to 3,500 teachers. At first, orders only trickled in, but even when they began to flow, the first years were hard. She bought a warehouse, and it caught fire. An employee embezzled money. Kolbe divorced her husband. In spite of everything, she never lost sight of her belief that there are no such things as problems, there are only opportunities. Today she grosses $3.5 million a year and Resources for the Gifted continues to grow.

American President Franklin D. Roosevelt was a cripple who had to be helped in and out of his wheelchair, yet he brought America out of the Great Depression and went down in history as one of the world's most respected and revered leaders.

Bob Hawke rose from the depths of alcoholism to become a major Australian labour leader and, eventually, that country's Prime Minister for four successful terms.

Wilma Rudolph was born poor and black in the Depression stricken Tennessee of the 1930s. When she developed polio at the age of ten, life didn't seem too promising for Wilma, yet she surmounted all these problems and went on to win three gold medals in track and field at the 1960 Rome Olympics.

The founding director of a successful investment firm in New Zealand shared with me his secret for hiring top performers. "We don't hire any senior people here unless they've had at least one major failure in their life. We find that people become more committed and determined as a result. It makes for a better person."

What opportunities are waiting for you right now in your life? You will never know until you look for them. Very seldom do opportunities stand up and wave a flag at you; they more likely come disguised as problems or failures. But opportunities do exist in abundance for all of us and, if you are willing to open up and explore your "problems" with this new attitude, some exciting surprises await you. Your struggles and stresses are challenges and opportunities. As Arnold Schwarzenegger says, "I believe very much in the struggle."

13.

Healing Ourselves

The mind is a great healer.
Hippocrates

CAN the mind play a part in determining a person's sickness or health? "What goes on in a patient's mind is often the key to whether he will get well," says Dr. Carl Simonton. Sitting in his office in the Cancer Counselling and Research Centre in Fort Worth, Texas, Dr. Simonton talks enthusiastically about the exciting new developments in treating disease with visualization techniques. The results he is getting are nothing short of fantastic.

"We think people are now beginning to realize how much the mind and the physical body are intertwined. Now we know it is possible for the cycle of disease to be reversed. We know that the same pathways that are used to transmit negative things, like cancer growth, can also be used to transmit positive things that can eventually restore a person to health. We are talking about some major changes in the way people view all illnesses and how they can cure themselves." Dr. Simonton and his colleagues are doing more than just talking, for his clinic achieves 3-4 times the average cure rate for cancer and he travels the country teaching other doctors how they can do the same.

In the last ten years, I have taught my mind power training seminars to over 20,000 people and I have seen incredible results, from people becoming multi-millionaires to winning major sports championships. These are impressive achievements, but most fulfilling of all to me has been my experience in seeing hundreds of people cure themselves of illness using these techniques. Let me introduce you to Martin Brofman. He can tell you his own story:

"In April, 1985, at the age of 34, I found myself in a hospital being told by my doctors that I had a tumor that was imbedded within the spinal cord. The tumor was malignant and I was diagnosed as terminal. I was told I had two months to one year to live. After several weeks of total despair, I decided to try and help myself.

"For 15 minutes twice a day I began meditating. On an imaginary screen in my mind, I pictured my body and the tumor. Each time I saw the tumor, I imagined it just a bit smaller than the last time I saw it. It was all in my mind, after all. I could imagine it any way I chose. I imagined that I could see the cancerous cells being dispersed by my body's natural immune system, and I told myself that they were being passed out of my body each time I went to the bathroom.

"Whenever I heard an inner voice suggesting that I was not getting better, I would quiet it, insisting that I was, in fact, in a state of improvement. I repeated to myself over and over while in this meditative state, "Every day in every way, I am getting better and better," until I believed it.

"In addition to the meditation sessions, I decided to reinforce my feelings of improvement in other ways. Each time I felt a strange sensation or pain in my body, instead of telling myself that it was the tumor growing, bringing me closer to my death, I told myself that it was "energy" working on the tumor, shrinking it, making it smaller and smaller, making me better and better. I looked forward to the sensations that I had formerly dreaded.

"All during the day, every day, I reminded myself of all the ways in which I was getting better. I imagined that the food I ate was "energized" making me healthier and healthier. I reminded myself continually of all the people who loved me, and I affirmed to myself that this love was energy I could put to use, to strengthen the healing process even more.

"I had no way of knowing whether all of these techniques were working or not, but I decided that if I felt better, they just might be. I had increasing mobility and energy everyday, just as I was telling myself.

"Two months after I began re-programming my mind, I was due for an examination by my doctor.

"The doctor was amazed. He found no evidence of a tumor at all. He could not believe it. This is exactly what I had visualized his reaction to be. I drove home, laughing all the way, to tell my wife the wonderful news."

This is far from an isolated case. There are countless examples of health being restored using similar techniques.

In the chapter on affirmations, I introduced you to Emile Coue and told you of the numerous healings he assisted by teaching his patients to focus their imagination on health with the affirmation "Every day, in every way, I am getting better and better." What you affirm to yourself, what you tell yourself, and how you talk to yourself play a vital role in what is going to happen to you. I remember once when I was teaching this to a group of students, a woman stood up and shared this story:

"Ever since I was a little girl, I have always said to myself, 'I'm the type of person who never gets colds.' I've always said that to myself and you know what? I never get colds."

The minute she finished a well dressed man in his fifties popped up. "This is very interesting," he said, "Because, you know, for as long as I can remember, I've always said to myself, 'Every year I'm good for one or two colds.' I've always said that to myself and you know what? Every year I get one or two colds." We all laughed, yet there is an important lesson to be learned.

In 1981, U.S. President Ronald Reagan was shot in the lung by an attempted assassin. This was quite a serious injury, especially for a man in his seventies, but I knew he would be all right the minute I read a report from a journalist who had interviewed the president on his hospital bed. Reagan had said, "Don't worry about me. I'm the type of person who always heals quickly." What a healing belief. How powerful.

Now let me ask you a question. What do you believe about yourself? Are you the type of person who says, "If there's a flu around, I'll catch it?" Do you expect to contract colds and flus and illnesses or do you believe you are the type of person who never gets sick? What you believe is going to happen has a powerful effect on what **does** happen.

In a set of experiments described by Jerome Frank, an authority on the placebo effect, you can clearly see how what you believe affects what happens to you. Test patients were given one of three different substances: a very mild painkiller, a harmless but ineffective placebo, and a heavy dose of morphine.

When patients were given useless placebos but were told they were getting morphine, two thirds reported that their pain disappeared.

When patients were given morphine but told they were getting a very mild pain killer, over half said they still had pain.

And when patients were given a harmless placebo which they had been told caused headaches in previous experiments, 3/4 of them developed headaches!

Whatever the patients believed was happening seems to have been more important than what was actually happening.

Medical authorities had already recognized the placebo effect, but this experiment went even further with some very interesting results. Unknown to the doctors, they too, were being deceived and the results were astounding. When the doctors administered a placebo under the impression that it was morphine, its effect on the patients increased. The experiment was then reversed and when doctors thought the morphine they were administering was a placebo, its effect on the patients diminished. Obviously, what the doctors believed influenced the results as much as what the patients believed. Now, how could what the doctor thinks possibly influence the patient? Isn't it what the patient thinks that counts? Or could it be that the doctor somehow subconsciously transfers to the patient his expectation of how the drug would affect him? If so, this is something to remember when a friend or someone close to us is ill. Our own attitude can be a valuable source of healing for both ourselves and others.

The body is a healing mechanism

Your body is a miraculous self-healing mechanism built to look after anything that happens to it. When you cut yourself, white corpuscles instantly rush to the spot to fight infection while the platelets congeal the cut and seal it up. It all happens automatically; you don't have to do a thing. Your body already knows exactly how to repair itself.

When you eat your body extracts nutrients from

the food and dispenses them as energy to various parts of the body, as required. It then discards the rest as waste and, again, it all happens automatically. You don't have to think about it or direct it. Break your arm, and you go to the doctor and the doctor heals your broken arm, right? Wrong. No doctor has ever healed a broken arm in his life. The doctor can align the bones to make sure they are straight, and he can put the arm in a cast to keep them that way, but only the body can heal them.

Remind yourself often that your body naturally heals and repairs itself. Insert thoughts of health and strength in your mind and you encourage it to happen. Affirm to yourself: "My body is a healing mechanism."

A two-minute health tonic

Every day spend several minutes bathing in thoughts of health and strength. Send these thoughts into your blood stream, your tissues, your cells. Imagine energy flowing through you. Experience your body as a miraculous healing mechanism. This exercise is an invigorating health tonic, and all it takes is two minutes of your day.

Your attitude makes the difference

When you first find out that you have a disease or illness the initial response is to panic. The mind becomes paralyzed with fear and the greater the illness the greater the fear. Part of the problem is that we see our disease as an alien entity or a "thing" rather than as a process. Wallace Ellerbroek, a former surgeon turned psychiatrist, says it eloquently: "We doctors seem to have a predilection for nouns in naming diseases (epilepsy, measles, cancer, tumors) and because we use nouns as names, then obviously they are things - to us. If you take one of these nouns - measles - and make it into a verb, then it becomes, 'Mrs. Jones, your little boy appears to be measling' or 'Mrs. Baker, you seem to be tumoring,' which opens both your mind and hers to the concept of disease as a process which comes and then goes." This is a more accurate way to look at illness.

Dr. Kenneth Pelletier of the University of California School of Medicine points out that the body can't tell the difference between a "real" threat and a perceived one. Our worries and negative expectations translate into physical illness because the body feels as if we are endangered even if the threat is imaginary. In other words, people who fear diseases are more likely to get disease because the body feels the effect of what is thought.

This phenomenon has long been observed in the area of conception. A Boston project, for example, found a 60 percent miscarriage rate in women who got pregnant soon after losing a baby to the Sudden Infant Death Syndrome. The report urged that such bereaved women "should wait until the body is no longer feeling the effects of grief." And how many times have you heard of childless couples unsuccessful in trying to have a baby until, finally, they give up and adopt a child? Within months the woman gets pregnant; the pressure to have a baby has been lifted.

Fun and joy can heal

It is no secret that depressed people become ill more readily than happy, easy-going types. Research has shown that stressful mental states like greed, anxiety, worry and fear can hinder the immune system's functioning. To combat this, several enlightened hospitals have set up "humor rooms" stocked with funny books, records, videos, cartoons and movies which patients can enjoy.

"There have been all kinds of reports in both folk and professional literature about people who have been cured or at least helped by the use of laughter and humor," says Shirley Routliffe, a Hamilton, Ontario therapist. Today, even traditional health professionals are making use of these findings.

Recent medical research into humor and health has shown that laughter releases two important types of hormones in the brain, encephalins and endorphins, which relieve pain, tension and depression.

Everyone is different

Dr. Patricia Norris of the Menninger Foundation, who teaches patients to use mind power to combat disease, tells the story of a nine year old boy who cured himself of a malignant tumor using a "Star Wars" visualization technique.

"Garret Potter was a terminal case - it was esti-mated he had only about six months to live. He had a virulent, malignant type of tumor. Radiation treat-ments had failed. Surgery was out of the question because of the tumor's location. If he fell down he couldn't pick himself up.

"Using his mind he visualized his immune system as powerful. It was a "Star Wars" like visualization-he saw his brain as the solar system and his tumor as an evil invading villain. He visualized himself as the leader of a space fighter squadron fighting the tumor and winning.

"Garrett used the technique for 20 minutes each night. At first his condition worsened and then it gradually began to get better. Five months later a brain scan was taken. The tumor was gone.

"The visualization technique was the only therapy employed after it had been concluded that the radia-tion therapy had failed."

Everyone is different. The technique which worked for Garret Potter may not be appropriate for everyone. Sometimes a gentler approach is needed.

Dr. David Bresler, director of the Los Angeles Pain Control Unit, describes a technique he used to help a patient. "The guy was in terrible pain, we'd tried everything we could think of. Finally, I decided to use guided imagery." Telling the man to take a comfortable position in an office chair, Dr. Bresler asked him to picture his pain as concretely as possible. The patient soon said that he could "see" a large vicious dog snapping at his spine. He was then asked to imagine himself making friends with the dog, talking to it. As he did so, the patient found his pain subsiding until, after a few sessions, it disappeared. Like many people he recovered his health only when he stopped fighting his illness.

Athlete Kevin O'Neal saved his career by using the power of his mind after a serious cycling accident. One of his hands was badly shattered and his confidence shaken just weeks before a major triathalon, but he visualized going inside his body and physically putting his broken bones together. As a result of his visualization, the bones healed twice as fast as expected and he was able to compete in the event.

The stories go on and on.

Dr. Paul Rennie of Vancouver, British Columbia, sums it up nicely when he says, "The mind is one untapped resource we have yet to fully explore. This is what we should be investigating," and no less an authority than Nobel laureate Joshua Lederberg has called this area "the most important step in medicine today."

Our health is our responsibility. We must take an active role in our health and healing. If sick or ill, we should not just give way to our illness, but should share in the responsibility for our treatment. When all is said and done, as Dr. Albert Schweitzer always proclaimed, "the real doctor is the doctor within."

14.

Prosperity Consciousness

To you the Earth yields her fruit,
and you shall not want if you
know how to fill your hands.
Kahlil Gibran
The Prophet

ANYONE desiring financial independence must first develop a "prosperity consciousness." Notice I said "develop" because prosperity consciousness does not happen by chance. No one is born with it nor can it be given to you. It is a state of mind tuned and vibrating to expect, acknowledge, and see prosperity and abundance everywhere.

The opposite of prosperity consciousness is "scarcity consciousness" and it's all most people know. Scarcity consciousness expects and acknowledges lack and limitation and sees it everywhere, searching it out like signposts on a road which seems to lead only to want, poverty, and hard times. No one will ever achieve financial success with a scarcity consciousness. It isn't possible.You cannot simultaneously travel both the path to riches and the path to poverty for they go in opposite directions. Both roads are clearly marked; there is no great mystery - whatever path you have chosen to travel will determine what will happen to you.

Do you have prosperity consciousness or scarcity consciousness? If you find you have scarcity consciousness, your task is clear. You must rid yourself of this mental ball and chain and develop the necessary prosperity consciousness.

There are five steps to follow in building a prosperity consciousness:

Step # 1:

Develop Prosperity Beliefs.

There are 4 main prosperity beliefs.

Prosperity Belief # 1:

It's an abundant universe.

Prosperity consciousness believes it's an abundant universe, that there is lots of everything for everyone if we but open ourselves up to it. Look at nature - lavish, extravagant, even wasteful in its abundance. Try and count the number of stars in the sky: you cannot, no one ever has or ever will; they number in the hundreds of billions. Look at wildflowers in a field spreading out far beyond what your eyes can see. Everywhere you look there is abundance. Likewise, in the marketplace opportunities exist everywhere if you focus your mind to see them. The only scarcity that exists is in our own consciousness.

Scarcity consciousness says "There's not enough to go around," "If I have a lot then someone else goes without," or, "If I get a promotion someone else misses out."

Scarcity consciousness believes that "everyone is competing against each other for the same things" and that "there are no opportunities," or that "there's very little money" and "everything is so expensive." Watch closely to see if you have any of these beliefs for it is a sure sign that scarcity consciousness has crept into your mind.

Prosperity Belief # 2:

Life is fun and rewarding.

Scarcity consciousness believes that life is hard and filled with problems and difficulties. Scarcity consciousness believes you have to work hard for everything you get.

I've met many people who believe "you have to work hard for everything you get" and they always work very hard for everything. How could it be otherwise with that belief? Remember what I said earlier about beliefs? The conscious mind will always give you ample evidence to support whatever belief you choose. Many people believe that life is harsh and difficult and, for them, it always is. Scarcity consciousness looks for and expects problems, difficulties, disappointments, and frustrations and it always finds them.

Prosperity consciousness looks at life as an adventure. It expects rewards. It looks for the fun and joy in life and always finds them. When problems and difficulties come they are seen as challenges and the opportunities that each contains are sought after and used. Prosperity consciousness appreciates life and knows with every new challenge comes greater rewards, new adventures, more fun. Life is full, rich, and rewarding, and new experiences and more success lie just around the corner.

Prosperity Belief # 3:

There are staggering numbers of opportunities in every aspect of my life.

Scarcity consciousness believes there are no opportunities around, that the best you can expect is what is happening right now. It tricks you into believing it doesn't matter what you do, that all the good ideas have been taken or that the time isn't right to start new ones. With scarcity consciousness the situation is always hopeless and there's never any point in trying.

Prosperity consciousness believes there are staggering numbers of opportunities in every aspect of your life staggering numbers! Not one or two or five or ten, but staggering numbers of opportunities. Where are they, you ask? Why, everywhere! Open up your eyes, **open up your mind** with prosperity consciousness and you'll quickly begin to see them.

Let me share with you a story which will illustrate this. Several years ago on Easter Sunday I got up early and hid ten small presents for the special woman in my life. The minute she awoke, I told her I had hidden some presents for her. She bounded from the bed, began searching excitedly, and after half an hour had found three presents. She sat down quite happily thinking that was all there were. "There's more than that," I said, which had her up in a flash searching for more. She managed to find two more and then, thinking there couldn't possibly be any more, she stopped looking. After lunch I casually mentioned, "Oh, by the way, I hid ten presents.""Ten?" she exclaimed in amazement and again began searching, going over the same area but this time really looking hard. She eventually found all ten but had I not told her there where ten presents she would have stopped at three fully believing she'd found them all. Likewise, if you believe there are no opportunities then chances are you will never find any. Why make any effort searching for opportunities that don't exist?

But if you believe there are staggering numbers of opportunities in ever aspect of your life, then you will actively search them out. Think about it!

Staggering opportunities for abundant health.

Staggering opportunities to make new relationships.

Staggering opportunities to advance yourself.

Staggering opportunities to become closer to your family.

Staggering opportunities to live a fun-filled life.

Staggering numbers of opportunities to make a great deal of money.

Let's look at making money . . .

I love the free enterprise system. I love a system that rewards ingenuity and imagination. Anyone can make a great deal of money if armed with the right ideas and the right attitude. The market place is an exciting phenomenon, dynamic and ever changing, seething with opportunities waiting to be tried. Tens of billions of dollars exchange hands every day. Money is in constant motion, flowing in every direction, so why not take your share by contributing to the system?

Each year in North America over 700,000 new businesses open. Every single one of them represents new opportunities for each will need printing, accounting, legal work, advertising, staff, maintenance, signs, office furniture opportunities, opportunities everywhere.

The United States, in 1940, had 10,000 millionaires. In 1980 the population doubled but the number of millionaires had mushroomed to 500,000. Opportunities, opportunities everywhere.

Never before in the history of civilization has there been an environment as rapidly changing as the one we live in today. Things are changing all the time and what is new and revolutionary this week becomes outdated in six months. This whirlwind environment means that opportunities are rapidly being created each and every hour. Every day there are thousands of new opportunities that didn't exist yesterday. Opportunities, opportunities everywhere.

Where are your opportunities? Jump into the action and find them; they surround you.

Prosperity Belief # 4:

Having lots of money is good.

It is my responsibility to be successful.

Scarcity consciousness believes that having lots of money is wrong, that you should only have enough for your basic needs, and that having anything beyond that deprives other people. Scarcity consciousness believes that successful people are selfish, greedy, neglect their families, and have their priorities wrong.

Prosperity consciousness believes having lots of money is good and that it is your responsibility to be successful. There is no question that the more money you make, the greater your potential for helping people, especially financially. It only makes sense: how can a philanthropist give a charity ten or ten thousand dollars if he hasn't allowed himself to acquire it in the first place? Money can be used in many ways to help and benefit those around us. Enjoy your prospects and help others to prosper, as well. When you are prosperous you can give to many charities, help friends, give to those less fortunate, create an immense amount of financial energy and direct it wherever you wish. It is your duty and responsibility to become successful, have lots of money, and help all those you can to prosper in their lives as well.

The first step in building a prosperity consciousness is to imprint the four prosperity beliefs into your
subconscious mind.

1) It's an abundant universe.

2) Life is fun and rewarding.

**3) Staggering opportunities exist for me in every
aspect of my life.**

**4) Having lots of money is good. It is my respon-
sibility to be succesful.**

STEP # 2:

**Look for and acknowledge prosperity in the *now*
of your life.**

You are prosperous right now if you open your eyes
and look for it. Don't wait for money to come your way
before you feel prosperous. Feel prosperous now!

**How I programed my mind for prosperity and
became wealthy**

Let me tell you how I first began programing my
mind for prosperity. I was living in a small cabin deep
in the Canadian woods with no electricity, no running
water, and no money, but I understood the principles
of prosperity and began re-programing my mind.

As I cut my firewood I would give thanks for my
prosperity. While stacking the wood I would say, "Not
one piece of wood, not two, not ten, but an abundance

of wood to keep me warm." When I ate my meals I would praise myself and the universe for the abundance I had. If I had a bowl of grapes in front of me I would count them one by one: not just one grape, not just two grapes, but an abundance of grapes. Walking in the woods I would see prosperity all around me: fields filled with thousands of wild flowers, trees everywhere, birds and wildlife in abundance. Nature was indeed bountiful. Even though I had no money I kept my mind focused on abundance. I knew that if I kept my mind focused in this way, the manifestation of abundance would soon follow.

When I gave my first public lecture, because I had very little money, I was forced to stay in a third class hotel. I was embarrassed about this and made sure no one saw me leave or enter. Often in the afternoons I would go into the lobby of a first class hotel to absorb the energy and vibration of the place. Soon I was making enough money to stay in first class hotels and I praised the universe for its abundance.

One day, while walking down the corridor of my hotel, I glanced into a room which was being cleaned and was amazed to see a large living room with no beds. I coaxed the cleaning lady to let me come in and look around and I was surprised to see that there were two rooms - a large living room and a separate bedroom. It was my first introduction to a suite. That day I began visualizing myself staying in suites until one day I finally rented one. I couldn't really afford it, but I wanted the vibration of wealth even if only to taste it for one evening. I walked around my suite feeling abundant. I sat down on the plush sofa and put my feet up on the table. This was real; I had made it to a suite even if it was just for one night. I praised the universe for its abundance. Gradually I began staying in suites more and more. At first I was making a little bit of money, then more, until lots of money was flowing my way.

Napoleon Hill, financial mentor to many great men, once exclaimed, "When big money begins to come it comes so quickly and in such large amounts that you wonder where it was hiding during all those lean years." It certainly worked that way with me. I still remember the day I realized I had really "arrived" financially.

It was at a party I was giving to celebrate my 5 year anniversary of teaching "Thought Dynamics." I was in Sydney, Australia, and staying in the Presidential suite at the Sheraton Hotel. It was a lavish suite - the living room was almost the size of the lobby. A huge glass wall ran from floor to ceiling across the entire suite and below me all Sydney lay at my feet: the opera house, the harbour, the sparkling city lights. It was a majestic sight.

I was entertaining my guests when I remember thinking, "what a change of fortune." I excused myself for a moment and went to the bedroom and then out onto the private balcony overlooking the ocean. In just five years I had gone from living in a cabin with no electricity or running water to entertaining my friends in the Presidential suite of one of the world's finest hotels. Not only that, but I had checked in for an entire month

- money was no longer an object. I thought back to how I first began programing my mind for prosperity and the fruit that it now bore and I thanked the universe for the secrets of success that had been revealed to me. I made a silent promise that I would pass these secrets on to others and then I rejoined my guests.

Begin programing your mind **right now** for prosperity. I began my prosperity programing in deepest poverty. There is no situation in which you can't begin prosperity programing.

STEP # 3:

Recognize and associate with success everywhere.

Everywhere you look there is success.

Everywhere you look there is prosperity.

Go to the centre of your city and look at the huge office towers. Think of all the success that is contained in just one of the buildings. You can be assured that the architect who designed the building made a great deal of money. The contractor who built the building probably made a small fortune. The owners of the building are obviously rich and successful men. The people who rent the lavish offices must also be successful. Now imagine how wealthy and powerful those who rent the top penthouse suites must be. Just that one building represents so much success and you can multiply that success by the number of buildings in your city. And that's just the beginning.

Never begrudge someone else's good fortune. Acknowledge it and feel good about it for it is proof that you can do it, too. Look for and acknowledge success everywhere you can find it. It is scarcity consciousness which resents success and tries to put down those who've achieved it. Guard yourself against these thoughts as if they were a deadly poison for they are, indeed, mental poison to your personal prosperity.

Always acknowledge and feel joy and happiness every time you see success whether it is your own or others. Open up your eyes and notice that success is everywhere, all around you, in abundance. It will be yours, too, if you adjust your thinking to prosperity.

STEP # 4:

Read inspirational books, listen to self-help tapes, join groups and organizations that desire success.

Everything you do becomes a part of you. This book you are now reading is filled with life changing principles that will make a tremendous impact on your life if you apply them. I will assume that everyone who is reading this book has taken my "Thought Dynamics" course. If for some reason you have not, make sure you know when the next one is being held in your city for the experience and information it provides cannot be experienced anywhere else. No book will ever duplicate it, not even this one. I know of no single experience that will help a person become successful more certainly than the four week "Thought Dynamics" course but drink from all sources - self-help books and groups, literature, sound advice - anything that inspires you to succeed.

STEP # 5:

Associate with succesful people both real and imaginary.

If you want to be a film maker, associate with other film makers.

If you want to be an artist, find other artists.

If you want to be successful, seek out the company of successful people.

The energy of success rubs off when you are in its company. Successful people think successful thoughts, make successful decisions, create successful plans, complete successful projects. You can pick up that energy and use it just by being in their company.

Let great men shape your life

All successful men and women have had their heroes and mentors. Sometimes these have been real people who guided and assisted them, but many times they were role models the individual knew only through magazine articles or books. You may never get to meet your heroes but let them inspire you, nonetheless.

A millionaire clothing manufacturer shared with me how, in her early years, she would emulate her business mentors. She had pictures on the wall of prominent women who had made it. Every time she looked at the pictures it inspired her to become successful, too.

Napoleon Hill also shares how he used great men from the past to assist him. He would create imaginary meetings with Abraham Lincoln, Luther Burbank, Thomas Jefferson, Andrew Carnagie, and Henry Ford - men whom he admired and respected and in these meetings he would discuss his business problems. Much to his amazement, these great men would advise him on how best to proceed. He credits much of his success to this system.

Did these men really advise him? Of course not, but the inspiration aroused by his imagination allowed high quality ideas and solutions to flow into his mind.

You, too, can have your success team.

Your responsibility is to succeed

You have to understand deeply that having what you want in life contributes to the general state of human happiness and supports others in creating success for themselves. Success never takes away from others, but rather, creates success for and helps others. The more successful an economy, the more opportunities exist for everyone. The more money you have, the more you spend in goods and services which create additional money and profit for other people to spend on goods and services, and so on.

Successful people help as an example and their success rubs off on everyone. You have a duty and responsibility to become successful for yourself, your children, your friends, and everyone who comes in contact with you. Everyone will benefit.

Your success helps many people. Your failure helps no-one.

Think about the above statement before you settle for anything less than success. Realize your success is more than just personal ambition, it is your responsibility. Don't be selfish, succeed. The world needs you!

Mind Power

15. Fulfilling Relationships

I will act as if what I do makes a difference.

William James

PERSONAL relationships are as vital to us as the air we breathe. We all need friends, lovers, companions, people with whom we can share our joys, sorrows, fears and successes. These interactions touch and nourish us at our deepest levels. We all need friendship, love, caring companionship, and a feeling of belonging, and yet often we remain distant and detached from one another, unable or unwilling to reach out and make meaningful contact.

We need new approaches and a greater willingness to explore the possibilities that exist in human interaction. If we choose, we can be a great source of growth and support for each other and strengthen ourselves in the process. Discovering how we can enrich and empower one another is an exciting turning point in our journey toward more meaningful relationships. We find that when we open up people respond and accept us for what we are. Instead of feeling vulnerable we become free, alive, vibrant, and awakened in ways we never experienced before. When this happens, every contact becomes meaningful, important, and enriching. What more could we ask?

Every person is a star

Every person is special, unique and deserves respect. **Every** person is a star. Your husband. Your wife. Your parents, too, are special, unique and deserve respect. Every one of your friends, your boss, your waitress, a taxi driver, a dying old man, the neighbour's boy-all are special, unique, and deserve your respect.

The realization that every person, no matter who they are or what their status, is special changes our attitude towards them. We now willingly grant them the respect they deserve. They may not know they are special or show it in their actions, but we know it, and treat them accordingly.

Learn to see beyond what people see in themselves. Everyone has the seed of greatness inside them and you empower people by seeing beyond their imperfections and problems to their potential, their depth, their inner beauty, and their possibilities.

I first discovered the transforming power of treating every person as a star while lecturing in New Zealand some years ago. I was travelling with an associate and his family. We had difficulty in finding a babysitter and had to settle for a woman who was one of the most negative and draining persons I had ever met. She complained constantly about anything and everything and whenever she arrived we tried to leave immediately so as not to have to spend too much time with her. I found myself thinking quite negatively about her and, catching myself, I decided to make some changes in my thoughts. I realized that deep down there was someone else inside, someone deeper and more joyous than the one we were seeing. I concentrated on picturing her in this way until I laughingly began thinking of her as "the ray of sunshine."

The next time she came over, instead of rushing out of the house I took her aside and said, "You know, every time you come into this house, it's like a ray of sunshine coming in." She looked at me dumbfounded. I went on, "We really appreciate you and your being our babysitter and we're happy that we have someone like you here." She was speechless. When we returned home later that evening, I again began praising her as "a ray of sunshine."

The next time she came over I greeted her with, "Look! The ray of sunshine is here," and I meant it, for deep down I knew that there was someone beautiful and wonderful there.

She smiled at me - the first time I had ever seen her smile. When the others left the room she said to me, "You know something . . . nobody has ever said something nice like that to me before. Never. Not in my whole life." I was stunned. Shocked. I couldn't imagine someone not having something nice said to them before. I wondered about her childhood and what misfortunes she had suffered through her life; what a hard life she must have had. I was glad that I had changed my thoughts toward her and ashamed at how I had previously put her down.

I continued to feed her positive, supportive energy and the result was startling. She stopped complaining, became pleasant - and almost amazingly - within weeks the lines on her face disappeared and she looked twenty years younger. Everyone noticed it. She actually became "a ray of sunshine." This incident forever changed the way I look at people.

When you recognize people as worthy of respect they tend to respond accordingly. You empower people by seeing the greatness in them. Maybe people don't see themselves as great and unique. Perhaps they feel worthless. Well, be their mirror! Show them that you see their potential. Show them with your acts, words, thoughts and feelings. Every person's life is important. Every person has a contribution to make. Treat each of them as special. Your support could well be the boost or turning point in someone's life, so don't let a person's outward appearance blind you from their greatness. Bring out the best in everyone by believing in them.

As you adopt this attitude toward people you will have meaningful relationships with everyone you meet and even a casual exchange will enrich both you and the other person. Our ability to help, love and share with one another is immense if we have the desire to do so.

Human: handle with care

We human beings are sensitive creatures. If you doubt this, look at yourself and see how easily you can be hurt or become offended. When wounded themselves, people hurt others. I discovered this by looking closely at myself. Whenever I was mean or hurtful toward someone else, it was always because I was suffering deep down myself.

Remember this the next time someone does something unpleasant to you. Ask yourself what pain might be inside them and feel love and compassion for them. It's no fun for them to be aching inside. We don't know what fears, scars, disappointments, insecurities, and difficulties people carry within them. As the old saying goes, "Don't judge a person till you've walked a mile in his shoes."

A woman who was taking my "Thought Dynamics" course was thinking of leaving her job because a co-worker was so thoroughly obnoxious. My student had built up strong dislike for this woman, in fact, the two were not even speaking to one another. Things had been like this for almost a year when she decided to try something different.

Realizing that perhaps her co-worker was unpleasant because of some deep inner hurt, my student began thinking kinder thoughts toward her and no longer let herself harbor her old resentments. Every time her co-worker was unpleasant she silently sent love to her. No longer did she react and get upset, but began actively empowering the woman, remembering that deep down the woman was special, unique, and deserved respect. She began a nightly program of visualizing the woman as being pleasant, warm and loving; she knew that, deep down, the woman was like that. She visualized herself and her co-worker as friends. Finally, one day she went over to the woman, apologized for not talking, and said she wanted to be friends. The woman was startled and didn't respond, but within days her mood changed. Now the two are friends and their working atmosphere is joyful and pleasant.

This happens all the time. I can't count the number of times I have heard similar stories from people who changed a relationship by changing the thoughts and attitudes they held toward the other person.

As you change your thoughts toward people, people change toward you

Because human beings are so sensitive to each other on so many levels, we are extremely receptive to the thought forms we hold about each other. If your relationship with your lover, friend, business partner, fellow worker, or parent is not what you want it to be, look closely at what thought forms you are unconsciously creating about that person. You may be clinging to and reinforcing the very qualities you dislike in them.

In relationships, as in everything else, we get exactly what we believe, think, and expect to happen. There are many possibilities in every relationship if you are willing to experiment with your thoughts. Visualization allows you to build new thought forms and become a creator in your relationships. Create, don't react.

Attracting the relationships we desire

How to attract the ideal mate:

STEP 1: Picture in your mind the type of person you want. What qualities are you looking for? Do you have a physical ideal? Visualize yourself with someone like that experiencing tender moments, sharing intimacy, laughing, having fun, going on outings. Create your ideal companion in the inner world of your thoughts. Don't try and put a face on this person or be **too** specific; let the universe supply it to you within the specifications you mentally imagine.

STEP 2: Focus on what you can give to this person. You have lots to offer. Feel good about yourself and think of all you have to give and share with that person.

STEP 3: Solicit the help of your unseen partner - your subconscious mind. Ask your subconscious to supply you with the ways and means to meet this special person. Re-read the chapter on intuition and follow the instructions and ideas your subconscious supplies you.

STEP 4: Contemplate these points: There are thousands of people who would love to be with you and share what you have to give. Your visualizations, affirmations, and intuitions are setting in motion forces which will bring you in contact with your ideal mate. Remember that that person is looking for someone like you, too.

How to attract business contacts

STEP 1: Picture in your mind the type of person you want to work with, and what contacts, skills, information, or knowledge you would like them to have. If you need a pearl diver fluent in Japanese, picture that. If you are trying to get a job as a freelance journalist, picture an editor with an assignment in your area of expertise or in an area that interests you. Visualize yourself with that person enjoying good rapport, a firm connection, and mutual receptivity to one another's proposals.

STEP 2: Focus on what you can give to this person, what talents, products, or expertise you can supply. Not only do you need them, but they need you and what you can offer.

STEP 3: Solicit the help of your unseen partner - your subconscious mind. Ask it to supply you with the ways and means of meeting this person. Re-read the chapter on intuition and follow the instructions and ideas your subconscious supplies.

STEP 4: Contemplate these points:

There are thousands of business opportunities and people who would love to have what you can offer.

Your visualizations, affirmations, and intuition set in motion energy and forces which will bring you in contact with these people.

A good affirmation is "I attract to myself the people I need."

Empowering others

We can empower other people with a minimum amount of effort on our part. In doing so, we strengthen both ourselves and the other person. Empowering people is a special and intimate way of touching others' lives.

Once, while waiting at an international airport, an announcement came over the P.A. system that my flight was canceled and that passengers should proceed to Counter 7 for further instructions.

When I arrived at Counter 7, there was already a sizable line and, as I waited my turn, I noticed almost everyone was venting their frustration on the harried ticket agent. People were anxious and furious over their missed connections and inconvenience, and demanding, "What are we supposed to do?" The ticket agent looked tired and drawn as she tried to explain the situation and her shoulders seemed to slump lower and lower with each new passenger complaint. When my turn came I decided to empower her. "I really appreciate all you are doing," I remarked sincerely. "I know this is a difficult situation and I know you're doing your very best. I've noticed how courteous and patient you've been with people and I know it's not your fault the flight is canceled." She sighed in relief that someone understood. I went on, "I just want to thank you and tell you I think you're doing a terrific job and I think you should be proud of yourself." "Thanks," she said, "I really needed that." After receiving her instructions I moved on, but happened to look back at her as she faced the next passenger. She was standing upright looking poised and confident. I had given her some needed energy. How simple and easy for me to express my appreciation, yet it made a real difference to her.

Can you empower people just by what you say? Of course! You can empower everyone you meet if you want to do so. You can empower the waitress after a meal, the delivery person, the taxi driver, the news agent, your children, and your friends by feeding them positive energy.

"We really appreciate the fine service you are giving us. You are making our meal a joy and a pleasure. You are a very good waiter."

"You are my favourite teller. I'm always pleased when you serve me. How has your day been?"

"Thank you very much!"

"That's an extremely attractive outfit you're wearing."

Even a simple "Have a good day!" if said with sincerity, enthusiasm, and a desire to make contact from your real self, will empower anyone.

You can also empower people without saying anything, using just your thoughts. A friend of mine likes to walk down the street silently sending out thoughts of goodwill to everyone he passes. A successful businessman I know silently affirms with everyone he meets, that they will have a happy and successful life.

Thoughts of love and acceptance free people. Kind words and encouragement inspire them. Acknowledging people strengthens them. Making people feel special, wanted, and needed empowers them. That simple effort can have results that can last for days, or even a lifetime.

Empowering ourselves

Sometimes we forget that the most intimate and closest relationship we will ever experience is with our own self. Be good to yourself; don't be too hard on yourself. Remember that you, too, are special, unique and deserve respect.

In the Bible it tells us to "love thy neighbour as thyself," and the emphasis is always on "love thy neighbour," but if we are to love our neighbour we must first learn to love ourselves. And if we want to love our neighbour more, then we must learn to love ourselves more. The more deeply you love and accept yourself, the deeper you can love and accept others.

Empower yourself so you can become strong,

loving, and healthy. **Acknowledge** yourself often and regularly. **Affirm** good things about and for yourself. **Visualize** yourself as successful, loving, open, and free. **Work** on your self-image and make it strong and confident. Like yourself. Love yourself. Be a good friend to yourself.

Nurturing our relationships

When was the last time you told a friend you loved them? When was the last time you thanked someone for their support, friendship, or love? Deepen your relationships by appreciating others and sharing that appreciation. "I really value and treasure our friendship," when said with feeling, can mean so much.

There are no greater riches in the world than friendship and human contact. Be a good friend to everyone you meet. Be there for other people. Accept people. Love people.Love unconditionally, whether or not they like or respond to you. Don't wait for others to make the first move. Open up. What have you got to lose except your isolation?

Transforming relationships means transforming ourselves

We are all members of the same universal family and, as such, must make ourselves available to one another in more loving, caring, and fulfilling ways if we wish to grow. The road to fulfilling relationships is a journey of change and growth. It means risking, exploring, and even stumbling sometimes. It starts with little things: a changed attitude, a reaching out, a look exchanged on a bus, a moment of total honesty with a stranger, but it soon grows into something much larger and more rewarding. It becomes a celebration, a joyful way of living in which we are open and aware in ways we never experienced before.

16. The Magnificent Payoff

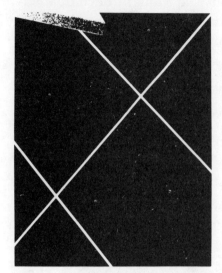

We all love to win but how many people love to train?
Mark Spitz,
winner of 7 gold medals,
1976 Olympics

READING this book is only the first formative step in developing and using mind power. No one truly understands the system or its benefits until they have practiced it for at least 30 days, and the **real** benefits emerge only after 60-90 days. Often noticeable changes do happen within the first few days or weeks but these are not to be confused with the lasting results that come with continued practice.

Above all, let the student remember that for steady growth, regular practice is essential. When a day's practice is omitted, three or four days' work are necessary to counter-balance the slipping back, at least during the earlier stages of growth. Better five minutes of work done regularly than half an hour on some days and none on others.

The vision

Nobody works without the thought of compensation. The Olympic athlete trains long and hard because the goal of a gold medal and the satisfaction of being the world's best lie before him.

An entrepreneur devotes his entire attention to his business because he reaps the fruit of his success.

A labourer goes to work each day because a paycheck awaits him at the end of each week.

A handyman spends his evenings fixing up the basement because he knows his efforts will eventually result in a cozy recreation room.

Behind all effort is the thought of the payoff, the fruits of the labour. If there is no compensation, then there is no reason or motivation to work; few of us work for the sheer love of it.

Do you have the vision of what training mentally will do for you?

If you think of mind power as "positive thinking" or "an interesting concept," or think "maybe it will work, and maybe it won't," then you will never make the effort necessary to train your mind. It is only the grand vision of what we can do and become that propels us to work regularly at creating our reality by these new and different methods.

There is a glorious life of power and opportunity awaiting you: it all lies within. Everything that you can conceive of wanting is within your grasp. The time is ripe and ready: are you?

Re-read this book carefully, studying all the principles. Train regularly and you will soon receive **The Magnificent Payoff**.

For all information concerning Thought Dynamics
courses, seminars, conferences, and audio and video
tapes, enquire at:

Zoetic Inc.
P.O. Box 38648
121 East 1st. Street
North Vancouver
British Columbia, V7L 4T7
Canada

Mind Power
P.O. Box Q379
Queen Victoria Building
Sydney, N.S.W. 2000
Australia

Mind Power
P.O. Box 27211
Mt. Roskill
Auckland 4
New Zealand

The French edition of this book is published by:
Les Editions de Mortagne
250 boul. Industriel
Boucherville, Quebec J4B 2X4
Canada